Morning has been all night coming

By the same author:

When you can walk on water,
take the boat

Morning has been all night coming

JOHN HARRICHARAN

Aquarian

An Imprint of HarperCollinsPublishers

Aquarian
An Imprint of HarperCollins*Publishers*
77–85 Fulham Palace Road,
Hammersmith, London W6 8JB

First published in the USA by Berkley Books,
200 Madison Avenue, New York 10016, 1991
Aquarian edition 1994
1 3 5 7 9 10 8 6 4 2

© John Harricharan 1991

John Harricharan asserts the moral right to
be identified as the author of this work

A catalogue record for this book
is available from the British Library

ISBN 1 85538 391 8

Printed in Great Britain by
HarperCollinsManufacturing Glasgow

SPECIAL THANKS

I am deeply grateful to my assistant, Anita Bergen, for her endless patience and constant encouragement. Without her help, I would still be typing this manuscript.

Special thanks to my agent, Bob Silverstein, who believed in me, even when there were times I found it difficult to do myself. My gratitude to my editor, Hillary Cige, whose suggestions made it a great pleasure for me to write this book.

Finally, special appreciation to my brother, David Harricharan, for his support and loyalty, to Sandra Matuschka for her comments and to the Three Himalayans for their continuous guidance.

CONTENTS

INTRODUCTION
by Elisabeth Kübler-Ross, M.D.

John Harricharan's new book begins where *When You Can Walk on Water, Take the Boat* leaves off. In a sense, it's a continuation, although, either one can be read independently of the other. When you read it, you'll love the style. You will see the ordinary life of an average man who becomes a widower and tries to raise two children by himself. He worries about making a living, taking care of the children, and still has time, in a way, to grow spiritually and emotionally.

If you have no problem with moving from one reality to another, from the physical plane to the spiritual plane, back and forth within a few pages, then this book is definitely for you. If you have problems with "reality testing," then you may have problems following this book with love, understanding and compassion.

Morning Has Been All Night Coming brought back numerous memories of talking to my own guides, of alternately existing in another reality, from the earthly level one to a higher one. The style of their communication is almost identical. They do not make life easy for you. They try to teach you. They do not give you answers, but parables, examples, and sometimes, perhaps, a hint of correction to your own interpretation of what you regard as painful or negative. This book brought back so many memories of my own experiences in different dimensions that sometimes I felt like crying and sometimes I felt like laughing. It was certainly the total déjà-vu experience from the first page to the last.

This book is filled with many points of interest, many gems of wisdom, many beautiful descriptions of our view of God and what we think of Him/Her. And naturally, there is the special experience of meeting God in person. It simply underlines that God is everything and everywhere and that when we become more perceptive and more open to this reality, we, too, will be able to have this experience.

Thank you, John, for sharing this book with us—those of us who are ready to hear and to see and to live; those of us who do not want to waste so much energy and time on trivialities, which will all be taken care of if we take care of ourselves internally, probably the hardest lesson to learn in the whole world. I'm still trying to learn it. Bless you, John, and thank you for sharing.

—Elisabeth Kübler-Ross

PREFACE

Some of us met on the pages of *When You Can Walk on Water, Take the Boat*. Others of us may have met at lectures, seminars, airports, by telephone or by letter. Still others may have met in areas beyond the more familiar, three-dimensional world. And yet, though our meeting may have been brief, as brief as two ships passing in the night, or as long as a lifetime, we are drawn together by gifts that transcend time—gifts such as truth, freedom, joy, peace, love and, most important of all, life itself.

And so, we meet again, or meet again for the first time, to unite once more in the glorious adventure of life.

Humankind has advanced tremendously from the days when our ancestors hunted the mammoth and danced under a full moon to celebrate the "glories of the kill."

If, perchance, there are other more advanced civilizations watching us, they might be intrigued by our progress. They might even remember the times, when in a less enlightened state, they, too, traveled our path and they, too, brought down fire and brimstone upon one another, even as we once did. Perhaps they will remember their struggles, and in remembering, will applaud our efforts and cheer us onward.

Yes, we have come a long way, but we still have a long way to go. Not only are we moving toward a greater tolerance and understanding of one another, but we are beginning to develop a greater reverence for all the other life forms with which we share the planet.

There appears to be a more enlightened consciousness on earth, and it may well be that we have begun to understand what the great teachers of history have been attempting to explain to us for centuries—that we are all children of the Infinite, that we are all on a journey home and that love is the most powerful force in the universe.

But sometimes, there is a high price to be paid for this growth and understanding—tears in the night, fears and guilt lurking in dark corners of your mind, and the constant pressures of everyday living. This is where we face our greatest battles—regretting the past and fearing the future. This is, also, where we can attain our greatest victories—living in the present. We are never alone, even though all our senses may be testifying to this "fact" and crying out in pain; even though it appears that hope has died and all we hold dear has been blown to the winds. There is a Presence and a Power; there is a purpose and a plan. And if we keep on keeping on, we shall finally prevail.

It is not by accident that we meet here. Nothing is ever accidental. We have met to learn from each other. Let us explore the infinite potential of our "creature-hood," and in the end we'll find that tragedy is but triumph turned inside out, that failure is only the other side of success and that all paths eventually lead to the mountaintop.

It is my privilege and joy to share with you, dear friend, portions of the story of our journey home. We are much alike, you and I, pilgrims in search for the peace and joy that have always existed in the "secret place of the Most High" under the "Shadow of the Almighty."

John Harricharan

CHAPTER
1

The Journey Home

Sometimes, the simplest things can be the most profound. So it was on this beautiful morning in June. It was almost like any other morning in summer except for the peculiarity of the sunlight in my backyard. The rays of light, streaming through the outstretched branches, seemed to take on a special hue. An other-worldly glow from these reflections set the tone for the day. What a glorious morning, I thought, as I made preparations to take my wife, Mardai, to the hospital again.

It had been slightly over two years that Mardai, only in her thirties, had been battling cancer; there were many things we were planning for the years ahead. The strain and stress of the disease had taken its toll on the two of us as well as the other members of the family. There had been a time when we faced life bravely and took no thought for the pitfalls that might lie in our way.

It is my belief that one can become accustomed to anything. Thus it was with our continuing fight with the disease. Over the years, the cancer had shown signs of retreating, only to return with a vengeance a short while later. Since Mardai had not been feeling too well recently, her doctor insisted on her returning to the hospital for observation.

As the time approached to leave, we said our good-byes to the children. Malika, our daughter, held her brother Jonathan's hand as we pulled out of the driveway. They are very special children, these two. Born approximately four years apart, they were both adopted at an extremely young age. They had brought much joy into our lives and now, at the ages of eleven and seven, were adjusting as best they could to the anguish of our family dilemma.

The hospital was perhaps an hour's drive from home. As usual, it was good to be alone with Mardai in the car. We spoke of the "good old days" and how kind they had been to us. We exchanged views on my work, the children, our friends and our future. Although she laughed at my feeble jokes, I could see deep within her eyes the shadows of sadness. With guarded expectations, we discussed plans for our twentieth wedding anniversary, which was only a week and a half away.

Our old car chugged along and we both retreated into silence for a little while. Suddenly, Mardai reached over and touched me on the shoulder. "John," she said, pointing ahead, "look at the letters on that truck." There in front of us, in the right lane, was a slow-moving truck with the large, black letters JH painted on the back. I guess that we all like to see our initials, and we laughed as we passed, and waved to the driver, who honked his horn.

Pulling ahead, I glanced through the rearview mirror and there on the front of the truck were the letters again. This time, however, they were painted in white. Mardai looked at me with the whisper of a smile and said, as more of a statement than a question, "I wonder what that means." A shudder ran through me as I heard a voice in my head say, "This is your last ride together."

What an awful idea, I thought. There, on the back of the truck, my initials in black. Up front, the same initials in white and, now, the worried feeling that something wasn't right. I was in the habit of looking for signs and symbols, even reading messages from license plates at times. I had found, as I mentioned before, that the simplest things could be the most profound. And yet, I never allowed myself to take any of these things too seriously, much preferring to maintain a balanced view of life, with all its seeming ups and downs. However, because I knew that everything in life has meaning and that we live in an orderly universe, I could not help but wonder about my current feelings and the possible meaning of the letters on the truck.

We drove on, both of us wrapped in our private thoughts. From the corner of my eye I noticed Mardai sitting quietly with her eyes closed. My apprehension grew. What if this was really our last ride together? No! That could not be. She was only a teenager when we were married. The almost twenty years we had spent together had seen their problems and their joys, but overall, they were the best twenty years of my entire life. What would it be like to spend the rest of my life without her? The prospect was unthinkable.

It is strange how one thought leads to another and, before you know it, you are left gasping from the most frightful of imaginings. It took a tremendous effort of will to break the cycle of doom and gloom that quickly overcame me there on the highway. But break it I did, as Mardai reached over, held my hand and sweetly said, "You are worried, aren't you, John? Don't be. Everything is going to be just fine." It was her way with me. She always seemed to know how I felt. Throughout some of the darkest days of the past, she would gently remind me that we would eventually triumph. I smiled as I nodded in agreement.

A few minutes later we arrived at the hospital and I parked the car. Though I knew she was in pain, she insisted on walking with me from the parking lot to the admissions office instead of using the shuttle service that was readily available. Finally, after a lengthy admissions procedure, we arrived at her room and unpacked her little bag of personal items. This was where she would spend the next few weeks and also where I would spend countless hours talking to her, reading, thinking and sometimes, in utter exhaustion, falling asleep.

The days bled together into a timelessness that made it difficult to tell where one ended and the next began. Back and forth to the hospital I went, sometimes twice, sometimes three times a day. My time was divided between working and visiting Mardai. Whatever little remained in between was spent with the children. I never tried to shield them from the seriousness of the situation, believing that honesty coupled with compassion was the best way to go. Children understand much more than adults give them credit for. Our two children, though confused and saddened at the traumatic turn of events, exhibited a wisdom and strength far beyond their years.

One morning while sitting quietly at Mardai's bedside, I was reflecting on the events that brought us there. She was sleeping peacefully. Startled by a feeling of others being present in the room, I looked around. I saw no one, yet there was a definite perception of great activity. The temperature dropped a few degrees and there were sounds like the rustling of paper. I sat quietly as I tried to observe. A slight breeze blew around me, and I thought I heard voices, somewhat muffled and distant, but seeming to come from within the room. Just as suddenly, it all disappeared and everything returned to normal.

It was only then that I realized that some major changes were occurring. I was scared of what might be happening. I had an ominous feeling that this was the beginning of the end. Mardai continued sleeping and again my mind wandered to long ago. I wished that my father were there with me in the room, but he had died a few years earlier. Even as I thought of him, I seemed to hear his voice say, "I am with you, son. I may be gone from physical earth life, but I am with you in eternity. We are taking care of things."

A tear came to my eye. Where was the help that we are told is always with us? There are times when one is so overcome with despair that even thinking requires a tremendous effort. This was one such time. Exhausted and worried, I closed my eyes for a short while. When I opened them again, Mardai had awakened. She looked at me ever so lovingly, ever so tenderly, and softly said, "I'm so worried about you and the children. I don't think I'm going to be able to win this time."

"We must fight a little harder," I said, trying to be brave as I held her hand and numbly sat there for what seemed to be an eternity. Then it was time to go home to the children.

Our twentieth wedding anniversary was spent in that hospital room. Mardai was somewhat happier as she smiled and handed me an anniversary card. I opened it, and there in her own handwriting were the words

"Honey, the past twenty years were my happiest. I pray God that He grant me another twenty years with you. I love you." She must have asked someone to buy the card for her. It was becoming more and more difficult for her to perform simple tasks such as writing. Her pain was becoming more excruciating, and even her breathing was tremendously labored.

Children were not permitted to visit the oncology wing of the hospital, but I thought that the next time I came I would bring Malika and Jonathan to see their mother. Tomorrow would be Sunday, and it would be a good idea to do it then, especially since it was a family tradition to spend as much time as possible together on Sundays. I told Mardai about my plan, and her eyes lit up with joy at the thought of seeing the children again. It had been over a week since she last saw them. We said good-bye and I left the hospital with a heavy heart. It was then that I understood the full meaning of the letters on the truck. The black letters on the back of the truck indicated that I would be going through extremely dark times, and the white letters in front meant that I would come out of the darkness into light. Little did I understand at that time how this would happen.

Sunday arrived and the children accompanied me as planned. Mardai was so extremely happy to see them. For some strange reason, the hospital authorities did not object to the children's presence. Mardai hugged Jonathan and Malika tightly and told them how proud she was of them. These were all signs of what was coming. Yet, I still refused to accept anything but total and complete healing for my wife. While much was being done by the medical profession to help Mardai, I knew inwardly that other methods, like old-fashioned prayer, could also help. It was time to take the children home, and so, again I left.

It is amazing how emotions can distort one's perception. Through my anguish it appeared to me that earth life was made for suffering and that one had to eke out a meager living, do the best possible and then die. In moments of desperation, that is how we think. But then again, when all around us seems to go right, we perceive the world as a lovely place in which to live, and we feel blessed to be a part of creation. Choosing not to remember our past problems, we fail to understand how others could suffer so terribly and we proceed blindly in our lives without much thought of suffering. I was feeling rather sorry for myself and this is always a sign to me of giving up. But it's not my nature to give up.

The next day, bright and early, I prepared to go to the hospital again. This time, I took only Malika with me, leaving Jonathan at home in the care of visiting aunts. The day seemed no different from many others, but I was beginning to sense a deepening river of sadness within me. A drive that normally took an hour lasted only forty-five minutes, yet I was not conscious of having driven faster than usual. Only a few days earlier, I had told a friend that whatever was happening was certainly increasing in speed.

As soon as we entered the hospital room, Mardai looked at Malika and commented, "What a pretty dress you have on." By this time, her pain was extreme and her breathing was more difficult than ever. Nothing seemed to be helping her. I left for a little while to take Malika back home, and when I returned, the situation had become worse.

Sometimes we feel that medicine can always perform miracles; at other times we want to damn the entire medical profession for its inability to help. On this, which was to be my last visit with Mardai, her parents and I stepped out of the room to confer with the doctors.

"There is really nothing else we can do," said the chief physician with a deep sigh. "We must now wait." A horrible emptiness overcame me. We had not come this far to lose. First, losing all our material possessions years earlier, then losing my father, and now the chance of losing my wife?* No! My heart screamed in protest, as if by sheer force of will I could change the course of destiny. No! She will again recover as she has done so many times before. But a still, small voice whispered, "John, you may say good-bye now."

I walked back into the room and looked at her sleeping so peacefully on the bed. They had administered some of the strongest painkillers to make her as comfortable as possible. Holding her hand, I whispered, "This is only a

*This story has already been told, in an earlier book entitled *When You Can Walk on Water, Take the Boat*.

blink in eternity. Wherever you go, I will find you." And then the tears came. Suddenly the room appeared to take on a brilliant glow accompanied by the sound of faraway music.

I became quiet. Leaning over, I kissed her on the forehead, stepped back, took one last look, turned and walked out of the room. A few minutes later, a doctor walked up to me, shook her head sadly and, with deep sympathy in her voice, said, "She's gone. I'm really very sorry." On that summer day far, far away from the little village where I was born, a light went out inside of me. The darkness deepened into a hideous void and I could no longer see the sense or purpose in living. Life seemed such a fragile affair, here one moment and gone the next.

Yet, even as I wept, a nobler part of me was already whispering the hope that every soul needs on its journey home. A part of me knew that from the depths of despair would emerge an understanding far greater than any I had ever known. In the days and nights ahead, there would be times of sadness, moments of loneliness and periods of reflection. But ever afterward, there would be a sense of purpose that would lead me on. Though no longer would I see her face or outer semblance, I knew that forever Mardai would be with me. I believe that we are all bound throughout eternity to that which we love and that neither heaven nor earth can ever separate souls who choose to be together. One soul might go ahead for a while, but the other always catches up.

Thus ended one phase of my life as another began. All endings lead to new beginnings. The closing of one door foreshadows the opening of another, and yet, at times, I wonder why there are doors at all.

CHAPTER
2

The Ancient Light Within

Among the different people whom I had met years ago was a man whose name was Gideon. Today, as I sat quietly on the porch gazing at the trees in the backyard, he came to my mind once more. Gideon was a very special person, indeed. I first met him in a parking lot not far from the Big City where I used to live. Together we shared some special adventures, and through him I was introduced to some of the most exhilarating experiences of my life.

I had often wondered what became of him. Through the difficult and trying times of the recent past, I always hoped he would appear again and share with me some more of the secrets of the universe, as he had done long ago. Both he and his colleague Marla had been a comfort during my times of financial stress, but it had been a long time since I had seen either one. The last time we met was somewhat like a dream. Gideon, Marla and I were at a party attended by some noted guests.

Time and distance take their toll on memory. I could vaguely recall mingling with the guests while listening to them explain their ideas about life on earth, God, the Universe and individual purpose. But that was a long time ago, and so many changes had occurred in my life since then. No longer did I share the company of my wife of many years. My children were growing up, and it seemed that Gideon and Marla dwelled in another time and space far, far away. Yet, there was an aspect of me that knew I would meet them again.

Days dragged slowly into weeks, and weeks into months. The emptiness that enveloped my life seemed to precipitate inertia: my only desire was to do nothing but sit and stare blankly. There are many things we know intellectually but do not believe in our hearts. What would it be like, I wondered, if Mardai appeared to me and told me how she was and what she was doing?

I am one of those fellows who has no problem falling asleep, and when I am asleep, there are very few things that can wake me. Thunderstorms, wind, music, lights— all have no effect on the quality of my sleep; yet, I would jump up from bed and be wide awake, within seconds, whenever Mardai called my name. Her voice did not have to be loud; just a whisper of "John" would do it.

One night, I went to bed around eleven P.M. and began to read. Feeling tired, I did not want to continue, so I put my book away. I must have fallen asleep immediately, because the next thing I remembered, I was sitting up in bed wide awake. Someone had called my name. I looked at the clock and it read 3:00 A.M. The voice sounded exactly like Mardai's, and instinctively I turned to look for her next to me, but alas she was not there. Could it be, I mused, that in moments of great stress, loved ones reach across dimensions to comfort and help us? There have been many recorded incidents of this nature, so I always tried to keep an open mind.

Perhaps Mardai was attempting to make contact with me. The voice was so real to me that I remained awake for a long while, alternately feeling joyful and sad. Although I felt a calming presence in the room, I neither saw nor heard anything else. Meandering through memories of Mardai, I finally fell asleep. And as I slept, I dreamed.

In the dream I saw Mardai in a small Caribbean village, the kind we liked to visit when she was alive. Dressed in a beautiful yellow sundress, she seemed to be no older than her mid-twenties, and though she smiled, there was an air of sadness about her. I walked up to her and said, "It's good to see you, honey!" In my dream, I knew that she had died. We spoke for a while, and then I said, "Where you are now must be so different from where I am."

"Yes, it certainly is," she replied.

"You must have access to so much information that we don't have," I continued.

"Yes, of course," she said sweetly.

"Will you help me to learn some of it?"

"Yes. I will be happy to do that," she said.

We began walking down a street that had lovely little tourist shops on both sides. We were chatting happily as we walked. Suddenly, we came to a point outside of town where the street divided into two, one side going on as if to the ocean and the other coming back toward the town. At this junction she paused, looked at me sadly and said, "I must go now. But look for Gideon. He will come to you again. Don't worry, for as you can see, I am well. No more pains. I love you. I'll see you again, soon." She was gone, and I was left alone taking the road back to town.

The dream dissolved, and I awoke with the feeling that something important was afoot. For the first time since Mardai died, I felt at peace. Yet, what did she mean by telling me to look for Gideon? Of course, I had been hoping that he would visit again. I could certainly use some encouragement at this low point in my life. And Gideon always had a way with words. His ability to illustrate a point with meaningful examples was extremely helpful. I strongly felt that a little help and guidance were in order.

Much as I would have liked to stay in bed a little longer, that was not possible. There were the children to look after and other matters to attend to, such as going to work. I did not like to leave Malika and Jonathan alone for long periods of time but occasionally this could not be avoided. It was not because of any special concern, but rather that I missed them while we were apart and was comforted by their closeness and the connection to their mother they provided me. After routine tasks were completed, I said good-bye to the children, left them in the care of their grandparents and drove to the office.

The memory of the dream was still fresh as I pulled up to a red traffic light. The Volkswagen model that looks like a bug is rare these days, yet I noticed a blue one to my right. I would not have paid it any more attention, but as the light changed to green and the bug started pulling away, I saw on the license plate the letters G-I-D-E-O-N. This was identical to an incident of this nature that had occurred years ago, just before my first meeting with Gideon. Then I remembered Mardai's message to "look for Gideon." Somewhat shaken, I tried to catch up with the blue "bug" and almost ran the next red light. But I lost sight of it.

Throughout the day I could hardly keep my mind on work, thinking about the dream, Gideon, license plates, strange coincidences, the children, dinner and myriad other assorted items. Deep within me was a feeling of growing expectation, and I found myself humming a childhood tune I had learned in the little village where I grew up. My reverie was interrupted by the ringing of the phone.

I picked up the receiver, and the voice at the other end

said, "Hello! I am an encyclopedia salesman. I would like to explain how you could own a set of our encyclopedia for only a small payment each month."

"I am sorry," I said. "I have no need for encyclopedias. I already have a couple of sets."

"A couple of sets? Do you collect encyclopedias?"

I was beginning to become annoyed. Actually, I did have two sets, the Americana and the Britannica. It was during my student days in college when I was approached by a salesman selling the Encyclopedia Americana. He convinced me that if I bought a set, he would win a trip to Hawaii. The cost of the books, he said, would be only a small down payment and a nominal sum every month. Even though I had very little money as a student, I wanted the poor man to win his trip to Hawaii, so I signed on the dotted line.

Three weeks after becoming the proud owner of a brand new set of Encyclopedia Americana, another salesman approached me on campus and told me that he was selling the Encyclopedia Britannica.

"I just bought a set of Americana a few weeks ago," I told him.

"Doesn't matter," he said. "You need to have both sets, and then you will never have to buy another set for many years to come."

"But I have no money," I protested. "And actually, one set of encyclopedias will suffice. As a matter of fact, I did not even need one, because the library has a set and I can use it whenever necessary."

"You mean, waste time to go to the library when you could have these books right in your own room? No, no. Your time is much too valuable. Only a small downpayment and a nominal sum every month.

"No sir," I said firmly, "I do not need or want another set of encyclopedias," and I turned to walk away. He rushed up to me and with desperation in his voice said, "Well, thank you anyway, sir, I guess we'll now lose the house. My wife will have to take the baby and return to her mother."

"House? Baby? Mother? What are you talking about?" I asked.

With a look of resignation, he explained. "You see, if I sell one more set, I'll get a bonus check that will pay my rent and prevent the landlord from kicking us all out. Really you were my last hope."

Was that a tear I saw in his eye? I stopped walking and studied him for a while. Only a beast would let such a poor man suffer.

"But I don't even have the downpayment," I said.

"It's only a small amount and you can mail it to me later," he quickly replied. "All you have to do is sign on the dotted line."

Perhaps some of us are born stupid while others acquire a good dose of it as we get older. I couldn't tell which category I fell into. In those days, however, being extremely naive in matters commercial, I dutifully signed on the dotted line, thus becoming the proud owner of two sets of encyclopedias. I rarely tell the story, because it is rather embarrassing. I swore I never wanted to see another encyclopedia salesperson in my life. And so I was less than civil when approached with this latest sales pitch.

"Well, I tell you what," he said. "Let me at least drop off a gift to you. What harm can there be in doing that?"

"Why don't you mail it?" I asked. "There is no need to waste your time bringing it. I assure you that I won't buy a set. My children have all the encyclopedias they need."

"Your address is . . . ," and he rattled off my address. I assumed that he had gotten it from some mailing list. There was an annoying persistence about him as he continued. "It will only take a few minutes. Please, let me drop it off. Company policy, you see."

"Well, what harm can there be? Only a few minutes you say?"

"Yes, I promise that I won't impose on you. This evening around seven P.M. Will that be fine?"

"Okay, I'll see you then," I said and hung up the phone. There was a vague familiarity in this conversation, a kind of déjà vu. It seemed as if I had heard every word he said in another conversation, years earlier. Well, this time would be different; no one was going to sell me something I didn't want! There is an old saying, "Fool me once, shame on you. Fool me twice, shame on me." I knew there was no danger that I would become the owner of three sets of encyclopedias; in fact, I was thinking of having some fun with the situation.

Returning home from work, I checked the mailbox at the end of my driveway. Just the normal stuff, except for a large, unstamped envelope, which appeared to contain a book. I greeted the children and sat down to examine the contents of the large envelope. I didn't recall ordering any books as I tore the envelope apart and pulled out a leather-bound volume entitled *The Ancient Light Within*. There was a yellow note stuck on the cover that read, "This is your gift. I'm sorry I have to cancel the appointment for this evening, but I'll be in touch with you soon." It was signed, "Your Encyclopedia Salesman."

Amazing, I thought. He only spoke to me a few hours ago, made an appointment, canceled it, and dropped off my gift in the mailbox. And what a title—*The Ancient Light Within*. Since I needed another good book to read, I was grateful for this one. I opened it and looked at the names of the publishers and the author. There, staring right back at me, were the words *"The Ancient Light Within* by the Editors of G&M Enterprises, The Big City, United States of America." On the left, inside cover, written in ink in beautiful penmanship, were the words "To John with love and the respect that one student of life owes another." The signature under that was unreadable. While trying to sort out this confusing information, I uttered an old expression I sometimes use, "What man! Blast!" The children looked up in surprise from their play, and Malika asked, "Is everything OK, Daddy?"

"Oh, yes," I quickly said as I put away the book.
Dinner first, I reasoned, book later.

After the children were in bed, I returned to the *The
Ancient Light Within* and flipped the pages. I was
familiar with the G&M company but wasn't aware that
they published books. The story was about a person who
became successful after a long series of tragedies. He
had followed the guidance that came from within himself
and had never given up. The hero's example was an
inspiration and a comfort to me.

Putting the book away, I thought to myself that
perhaps we all have the ability to turn disaster into
triumph and poverty into plenty. Perhaps within us all is
this "ancient light" that will guide us if we just look for it
in our hearts. With disconnected thoughts of that nature,
I turned in to bed, forgetting books, forgetting encyclopedias, forgetting everything but the soft comfort of my
pillow.

Tomorrow would be Saturday and I so looked forward
to weekends.

CHAPTER
3

The Return of Gideon

When I awoke it was already daylight. I have a favorite spot where I sit with my first cup of morning coffee. It's in the kitchen, facing the large window that overlooks the woods behind the house. Earlier that year, I had erected a number of bird feeders, and I took pleasure in watching the birds as they enjoyed the seeds Malika and Jonathan set out for them. One bird feeder was suspended from a thin wire stretched out between two giant oak trees. This I had done in my never-ending battle to prevent the persistent squirrels from devouring all the birdseed.

Squirrels are relatively intelligent, it seems. In spite

of all my precautions, they always found a way to get to the feeders. This morning I observed two young squirrels eagerly eyeing the hanging feeder. I could almost feel the intensity of their focus as they appeared to be mentally calculating distances between the tree and their goal. Finally, one of them jumped, bumped against the feeder and tumbled to the ground. In so doing, he shook some seeds off the feeder, and he and his friend started eating the fallen seeds. They rotated the procedure, each one taking a turn at jumping and hitting the feeder, then both of them feasting on the seeds.

There seemed to be no conflict in their systematic performance of this practice, no competition, just cooperation and sharing. As I got to thinking, I forgot about the book I had received in the mail, I forgot about the problems I still had to solve, and I wondered who had taught the squirrels their acrobatic feeding routine. How did they learn to bury nuts? What was the life force and the intelligence in them that made them so graceful as they went about their daily tasks? There is an unhurriedness about animals that is so uncommon in most human beings. They seem to live entirely in the present with no regrets of yesterday or any fears for tomorrow.

But my thoughts went back to *The Ancient Light Within*. Isn't it strange, I asked myself, that an encyclopedia salesman would give me such a book? Somehow the thought of my old friend Gideon popped into my mind. I had the feeling that he was close and that I would see him soon. I remembered that distant day at the party

where he and his friend Marla had waved good-bye to me
as they said that they would always help and keep in
touch.

The phone rang and broke my train of thought. Why
would anyone call so early on a Saturday morning? The
children were still in bed, and I was enjoying my coffee,
my birds, my squirrels and my reflections. Reluctantly
and with some annoyance, I picked up the receiver. It
was the encyclopedia salesman.

"Hello, Mr. H. I trust it's not too early for you. Did you
receive the gift I told you about?"

"Yes. Thanks, but couldn't you call later? It's so early.
The children are still in bed," I said.

"Just wanted you to know that we have a special deal
just for you," he answered as if it were a totally normal
thing to call a stranger before seven o'clock in the
morning. "I really am sorry. But I feel that you are a
very busy man, and I wanted to get in touch with you
early. I have some exciting news for you."

"Please. I told you before that I'm not interested.
You're wasting your time," I said, not wanting to be
rude. In years past, I was involved in the sales field and
had developed an empathy for salespeople. I had culti-
vated a great appreciation for their courage and persistence as they went from rejection to rejection until they
made a sale.

"This one time, sir," he answered. "Let me stop by and
explain to you the terms and conditions for picking up
the prize you've won."

"Prize? What prize?" I blurted out.

"Yes. You see, you were the thousandth person. I mean, you were the one thousandth name I picked at random to call. Our company's policy is that we give a free set of encyclopedias to each salesperson's thousandth prospect. You are one in a thousand, Mr. H. Now, may I stop by to tell you all about it? I'm only within ten minutes of your home."

The voice on the phone sounded so charming and full of integrity. How could I resist? Perhaps there was a catch to this, but I finally gave in, resolving to be cautious. "Okay. I'll see you in ten to fifteen minutes. Do you know how to get here?"

"Of course," he answered. "Remember, I dropped off your free gift yesterday. The book in your mailbox? Thank you, Mr. H. I'll see you shortly."

Somewhat elated because I had actually won something, I poured myself another cup of coffee as I awaited the salesman. I had not even thought of asking his name, and I did not recall that he had mentioned it to me. Anyway, spending half an hour with him would not be a problem today. The children would be in bed for another hour or so, and we had nothing special planned until the afternoon. I put on a fresh pot of coffee, cleaned up the mess in the sink, checked on the birds and the squirrels once more, then picked up the book that the salesman had left the day before. As I flipped through the pages again, the doorbell rang. I put down the book, walked over to the front door, opened it and said, "Hi! . . ."

That was all I could utter as I stood there gaping. Standing before me was a bearded man in a dark blue business suit. His hair was as black as a raven's wings, and his eyes were filled with laughter. He seemed not to have aged one bit since I last saw him, many years ago. I must have been a study in marble as I stood there trying to mumble something sensible. He noticed my predicament and said, "My goodness, John, aren't you going to ask an old friend in?"

"Of course, of course," I said, as I gave him a big hug. "Come on in. I should have known it was you. What are you doing selling encyclopedias?"

"Let's sit down and I'll explain. I smell fresh coffee. Do you mind if I have some?"

We walked into the house, and he sat down as I poured him a cup of his favorite brew. I felt an overwhelming sense of joy at seeing Gideon again. It was he who had stood beside me, comforted me, taught me and helped me during my years of tribulation. I had never forgotten our times together, but I always wondered what had become of him and Marla. Where were they when my wife died?

"I can already hear the thousands of questions in your mind, John," he said as I handed him his coffee and sat down.

"Where have you been all this time, Gideon?" I asked.

"Fulfilling my assignment, John" was his answer.

"Your assignment? What assignment? Selling encyclopedias?"

"The selling of encyclopedias was the method I used to make contact with you again," he said. "But it was more than that. We were also checking to see how your understanding had grown. Even with your busy schedule, would you, without giving a poor salesman a chance, turn him down? Had you learned patience and compassion? Would you give me or any other fellow human being a few minutes of your time or would you be so self-centered that you would not be bothered? We needed to have some of these questions answered."

"You mean you were testing me? That wasn't necessary. I've been through quite enough tests in the last few years, Gideon."

"Quite so, John," he replied. "But tests don't care. They just turn up and say, 'Look! I'm a test. You may do with me whatever you like. You may ignore me if you want to or deal with me as you see fit. I'm just another one of your tests.' That's what tests say. You yourself have designed them for your own private purposes, to measure your current progress against your potential. Actually, they are meant to bring out the very best in you, but of course, that doesn't always happen."

Gideon was very serious as he spoke. You would think that our conversation would have been on a lighter note since I hadn't seen him in such a long time. He still had not explained where he had been. His habit of answering a question with a question, his ability to turn a statement into food for thought fascinated and frustrated me at the same time.

"I see that you are your same old self, Gideon, still able to turn even the simplest situations into learning experiences. Don't you think we have had quite enough dialogues about life and tests and should really be enjoying each other's company again?"

"There is much to be done now, John. That's why I'm here."

"Really, Gideon, where were you all this time? And please don't tell me about fulfilling assignments."

His face took on a sadder look as he leaned forward. "I have always been watching you, John," he whispered. "I have sat with you through your agonies and have cried tears with you through your sufferings. I was with you in that hospital room as much as I was with you when most of your friends and family turned away from you. I rejoiced with you when you were happy. Yes, John, I have been with you all this time."

I was puzzled and annoyed. He was with me all this time and never lifted a finger to help? As if reading my thoughts as he used to do, he said, "Although I—and others—were with you, we were not permitted to interfere. We have rules, too, you know."

I found myself becoming more agitated as I spoke. "Look, Gideon, you and others, like Marla, amuse yourselves flitting through time and space. You seem to have extraordinary abilities, like appearing and disappearing at will. With the flick of a little finger you can solve someone else's problem, and yet, you have the nerve to sit here and tell me that you were just watching me?

Standing by while I went through agony? Well, I hope I put on an entertaining show for you, my friend."

"You are becoming upset, John," he said, hardly raising his voice. He always amazed me by remaining calm in any situation.

"Upset? No, not really upset, only terribly disappointed that you did not use any of your remarkable abilities to help me out of some of the worst times of my life. I'm just—"

He did not let me finish but interjected quickly, "We are not always permitted to jump in with what you call special talents and solve everyone's problems. Even we have to remember that when you can walk on water, it might be advisable to take the boat. If you, as a father, always stepped in and solved all your children's problems, how would they evolve and grow? How would they learn to be independent, fulfilled beings with the ability and desire to contribute to your world?"

His logic was irrefutable. I calmed down somewhat. "Yes, yes. I know. Sometimes for the greater good, we can't interfere in the learning process and all that. But once in a while, Gideon, just once in a long while, I wish you helpers of humankind would stretch forth your hands and do something, a miracle perhaps, that would assist an unfortunate pilgrim along the way."

He had just taken a sip of coffee as I was speaking. At my words, he slowly put down his cup and looked at me. His eyes, full of both sadness and understanding, burned into mine. "That is precisely what we have been doing for you, John," he said.

"You mean, Gideon, that you have been helping me all this time? My whole world shaken up and everything falling apart and you have extended a helping hand to me? Good heavens, man! I wonder what it would have been like if you *hadn't* helped me. Look, perhaps I feel a little too sorry for myself once in a while. But, surely, you must realize that we do get tired fighting the battles of life day in and day out."

He nodded as he answered, "Yes you're tired, but you have a few of your facts mixed up with your opinions and perceptions of things. Life is not a battle. That is your first mistake. Look at it as a battle and you have no peace. Life is not like a roller coaster. Look at it as that and you will always have ups and downs. Certainly you've been through much in the past years. Of course you and others with you have suffered. But that is only part of the story. Believe me, you were watched over and you were protected. All people are. Each and every one of the human life forms on earth has its own protective system. You are forever safe even though at times you may think that your world is crumbling."

Almost an hour had passed while we sat there talking. I was still curious about many things; I shifted the direction of the conversation. "Gideon, tell me about G&M Enterprises. Do you still work for them? And Marla, how is she?"

"All in good time, John," he replied. "One phase of your life is over and another has begun. We have to work much more closely now. That is why I am here today. I

will have to leave soon. But I will be in touch with you
again. Just read and reread the book I gave you. It is
somewhat like a tour guide, and provides pointers on
how to navigate the oceans of life. You'll enjoy it."
Gideon leaned back in his chair and looked at the clock on
the kitchen wall.

"Don't tell me you are leaving now," I said. "You just
got here. I need answers to many questions."

"No, John. You have the answers. What you need to
work on are the questions. Start asking the proper
questions and you'll be amazed at the brilliant answers
you have."

"There you go again," I said. "Always delivering
statements with many meanings. Gideon, I have missed
you and I hope I see you more often. By the way, would
the children be able to see you if they were here in this
room? You remember that long ago, no one else could see
you but me?"

"Only if it's necessary," he replied, getting up from his
chair. "They'll see me eventually. So will others, too,
when it's appropriate."

"When will we meet again?" I asked, reluctant to let
him go. There were so many things to discuss. For
example, I wanted some explanations as to why Mardai
died at such a young age.

"Sooner than you think, John," he said and then as an
afterthought continued, "Of course, you will come to
understand more about your wife's death and your future
work, which, even now, has already begun."

Gideon came over to me, shook my hand and then walked toward the door. I showed him out, and as he went to his car, he waved once more. It all felt somewhat like a dream. Here he was again, and yet I was as calm as if it were a totally natural thing for the Gideons of this world to pop in and out of our lives. I could now hear the patter of feet and knew that the children were awake and would be down for breakfast shortly. I wondered what they would have said had they met Gideon. I was to find out in an amazing way within the hour.

CHAPTER
4

Where Does the Butterfly Go?

Malika came down first. As is customary in our family, she walked over to me, kissed me good morning and sat down at the kitchen table. Jonathan immediately followed. There was the usual light in his eyes as he smiled.

"Hi, Dad," he said. "Was somebody here? I thought I heard voices."

"Oh, just a fellow who was passing by," I replied.

"The one who said you won a set of books?" he asked.

Taken aback, I asked, "Who told you that?"

"I'm not sure," he answered. "I had this dream last night and Mommy told me in my dream that a man was coming to see you and he would bring you a set of encyclopedias. The dream seemed so real."

Malika sat quietly listening to our conversation, and then she jumped in. "Dad," she said. "Do you remember that man called Gideon? You used to speak about him. Well, I, too, had a dream, but it was about Gideon."

"What did you dream, honey?" I asked.

"Well, it doesn't make much sense, Dad," she said. "Something about books, I think."

"Tell me anyway," I replied.

"OK. But I think it's nothing. Jonathan and I were playing by the swings at our old house near the Big City. This man came up to us and said that his name was Gideon and that he would be visiting you and helping you with your problems. He also said that you were very tired but that all that would soon change. He will be bringing you a set of books and he wanted us to tell you that."

"Dreams," I half mumbled. Now my children were dreaming of Gideon, and on the same day that I saw him. For most people life seems a bit confusing. In this respect, I was no exception. I was extremely happy to see Gideon again, but at the same time, I was puzzled by the children's dreams. I had a feeling that even my children were trying to bring me messages of comfort.

I dismissed thoughts of Gideon for a while, and we enjoyed our breakfast. A busy day followed until finally it was evening. The children went upstairs after dinner and I was left alone with my thoughts. As I sat on the back porch looking into the woods, I enjoyed the sounds of the tiny birds as they flitted back and forth over the bird feeders.

It was a lovely evening, neither too hot nor too cold. A gentle breeze lent a quiet peace to the surroundings, and stars were shining in the sky. Far away above the trees a few clouds were lazily making their way home. "Home?" I mused. "Where do clouds go when they return home?" Given to philosophizing at times, I followed the thought. Clouds go home to the oceans of the world. They become one with what they have always been. A cloud, it seems, is the ocean expressing itself another way. Perhaps, I, too, came from an ocean of being and was expressing myself as John. A cloud only changes form. It never dies; it only changes. It may disappear for a while only to reappear again in a different form in a different place and time.

Those thoughts led me into thinking about Mardai. Where did she go after her transition? I consider myself somewhat open-minded and even a bit enlightened. Yet, there are those moments when I hurt a lot and do want to ask such questions. Was she called away, or did she go of her own choosing? We all know where the caterpillar goes. It leaves itself to become a butterfly. But who can tell where the butterfly goes?

Because I knew deep within my heart and mind that life is much more than it appears to be, I felt an inner strength and guidance. I was able to survive the devastating blows of the world of commerce and trade. I was able to live with seeming loss, always knowing that, in reality, one never loses. On some level of consciousness not quite apparent to me, I accepted all setbacks as challenges.

Then the voice came out of the darkness. A gentle, loving voice, neither too loud nor too soft. "John," it said, "it is in being the caterpillar that you become the butterfly." I looked around but saw no one. Yet, the voice continued. "And it is in being the butterfly that you know where the butterfly goes."

I stood up and peered into the woods. By this time darkness had descended. I was puzzled by the voice, and I had started to think that I might have been imagining answers to my questions when I saw a small pinpoint of light moving in the darkness. "Fireflies," I said, as the light became brighter and brighter. "Actually, a bunch of fireflies!" I knew that fireflies did not fly in groups, yet I stood there fascinated by the performance. Strangely enough, I was neither excited nor apprehensive as the glow continued. By now it was as bright as the beam of a flashlight. Then it stopped moving, as I continued staring.

It must have only been a few seconds, but it seemed to be forever as I was bathed in the radiance of an otherworldly phenomenon. Suddenly, just as it had started, it stopped. One moment it was there and the next moment gone. Out of the darkness I heard footsteps, and as I turned to look in the direction of the sound, up walked Gideon.

"Bet you didn't expect to see me so soon," he announced.

"You must stop doing things like that, Gideon," I said after I caught my breath.

"You mean the light?" he asked somewhat innocently.

"Not only the light, but the voice and your sudden appearance," I replied. He had a habit of instantaneously appearing at the strangest times.

"Well," he said, "I was sure that you'd be used to these things by now. May I come in and have a cup of that coffee you make?"

"The children are upstairs playing a video game. What if they come down and see you?" I asked.

"Don't worry about it, John. They have already met me. Didn't they tell you about their dreams?"

"Oh, so that's it! That's why they told me about their dreams and your set of books this morning. Hardly anything you do should surprise me anymore. By the way, old friend, where is the free set of encyclopedias you said I won?"

Gideon's face lit up. From what I knew about him, he rarely, if ever, became excited about anything. This time he showed a flicker of emotion as he said, "I am glad you mentioned the books. You will receive them soon. And as for the children, they understand much more than they are given credit for. Now can we go inside and have that coffee?"

Over a hot cup of coffee, I looked at Gideon. Still the same beard and still the same eyes. It seemed to be yesterday as we sat there. I was fully determined to get some answers to questions that had puzzled me for some time. He was quiet for a while, as if thinking about what to say. I broke the silence. "Gideon, whatever happened to Marla? Will she be helping me too? Does she still work for your company?"

"Yes. You will meet her again. She has additional responsibilities these days. But we will let her explain what she does when you see her."

"When will that be?" I asked.

"All in good time" was all he would say.

"Do you remember the time a few years ago when we were at that special party? It seemed as if we met people from different times and places. Do you recall how we seemed to travel back in time? Do you remember any of those things?"

"Of course, I do, John. You're the one who forgets so quickly. There were situations that you yourself referred to as miracles, and yet, you forgot them. You were supposed to remember those times and to draw strength from what you saw and heard." He became more intense as he continued. "Sometimes, although people might see the moon turn blue or someone walk on water or through a fire and say, 'That's amazing,' in a short while they forget. There's a tendency to remember only the bad times and discount the good things that happened, to get caught up in the problems of life instead of the joys of living."

"Gideon, so we don't waste any time, why are we

discussing these things? Why don't we go on to more practical matters? I certainly would like some advice on my personal situation—for example, my finances."

"First of all, you couldn't waste time even if you tried. Actually, time will waste you if you don't utilize it properly. And as to advice on practical matters like finances and other seemingly mundane things, let me assure you, those things spring from the deeper parts of your being. They are only a reflection of where you have been and of who you are. Fix the internal thinking processes first, and all the external worldly things fall into place."

"I understand all that. 'Think and Grow Rich,' 'You Create Your Own Reality,' 'As a Man Thinketh,' and dozens of others. Lovely sayings, of course, but to put them to work in your life is, most times, more easily said than done."

"But it *can* be done and is *being* done by many on earth today. It's just a matter of following some simple rules."

"Gideon," I finally said, "I'm really not interested in philosophy or concepts today. As a mental exercise, I imagine these things can be fun. But I'm more concerned with the practicalities of everyday life, not with a lot of pie-in-the-sky concepts."

"That's why I'm here," he said, pulling a little black notebook from his pocket. "Let's see what we have. Yes, the schedule shows we will meet again soon. Perhaps you will understand more by then."

"Listen, Gideon, I do like and appreciate you, but I'm

tired of spending time on all these esoteric subjects. You don't have to raise two children and earn a living, all at the same time."

"First of all," he said as he stood up, "you don't have to spend time, you only have to spend thoughts. And secondly, you do not raise children. They are not crops or livestock. You just have to love them, teach them and lead by example. We will go into more of this later. I must leave now."

Gideon smiled and walked to the door. As he opened it and left, all I could say was, "See you soon." And then he was gone. I went back to the table and finished my coffee. Then I went upstairs to see what the children were doing.

CHAPTER
5

The Transformation

Sunday morning arrived, and Gideon was but a memory for a while as I busied myself with the normal chores of daily living. Later on, I went for a walk and got to thinking about the past few years, about Gideon's comments on how we are almost always forgetting good things and remembering bad ones. It seemed that was just the opposite of what psychologists had been saying. I was taught that we tend to forget our unpleasant experiences and remember the good ones. Yet, how many of us always focus on what might have been, what got away or our failures rather than our achievements.

I had learned so much from Gideon and had put so

little of that to use. I, too, was guilty of not counting my blessings. According to him whatever we focus on becomes our reality. Perhaps by looking too closely at the difficulties of the past, I prevented myself from seeing what could be. I resolved then and there to do my best to change the way I looked at things.

All of a sudden the realization came to me in a brilliant flash of insight. I was safe. The children were fine. We were all healthy, and there had been enough money in the past to keep us going. Malika and Jonathan were doing extremely well in school. I had totally changed career directions and was now writing articles for magazines, lecturing, and consulting. I had even had a book published and was writing others. No one had repossessed my car, the mortgage was up to date, my new friends were extremely supportive, and even relatives seemed not to be as bothersome as before. Actually, things were going well, with the promise of becoming even better.

Why, then, did I worry so much about everything? A friend had once commented to me that it appeared I had forgotten what it was like to be happy. And now, as I pondered all these thoughts, it became clear to me that worrying was a habit and, by the same reasoning, being happy was also a habit. It was just a matter of choice. Experiences in life do not create our emotions. Rather, our emotions have a great deal to do with creating our experiences.

Here I was, putting the cart before the horse. I began

to remember some of the simple rules of life that Gideon had reminded me of: live one day at a time; do the best with what you have; love and help one another. In remembering I became extremely elated. The joy of these recollections generated considerable excitement in my mind, and before I knew it, everything seemed well with the world. It was as if I had just taken off dark glasses and was finally able to see clearly. I had been living in the past but had not actually been brilliantly alive in the present.

I continued my walk, noticing things that I hadn't noticed before. The trees seemed to be more alive, the flowers more beautiful, and I was aware of butterflies floating gently around me. A passing motorist waved and smiled. I picked up a pinecone and tossed it with unbounded pleasure at a lamp post—something I hadn't done in years. I felt vibrant and at one with the world.

I reached the point where I usually would have turned around to walk back home. I stood there for a moment and looked up at the sky. How blue and beautiful, I observed, with clouds chasing one another across the span. The wind ran races through the growing grass, and way off in the distance I could hear a dog barking. There I was, in the center of a whole new world that was not really new at all. I looked at my hands and feet, felt the sweat on my brow and realized that all my physical being was just a part of the universal scheme of things. There was order in the world and order in the universe, and even though at times the order might be disguised by the

pressures of everyday living, it was there—gloriously—
every moment of our lives.

No worry came to me as I retraced my footsteps.
There was music in the air and I was a part of it. Life was
meant for rejoicing, not for suffering. Focus on suffering
and that's what you get—more suffering. Be alive all
your life, strange as that sounds, and you find that planet
earth can be a lovely adventure. So many years I had
spent in worrying about money, illness, family and
everything else, that I had lost sight of some of the more
important aspects of life—joy, peace, quiet and understanding.

Creeping over me was a feeling of embarrassment for
knowing so much and doing so little. I, who had learned
such valuable lessons about life from Gideon, how could
I not have put that learning to practical use? However,
self-recrimination is as dangerous as chronic depression.
It creates guilt, and guilt is perhaps one of the deadliest
enemies of humankind. Guilt's only message to us is,
"You don't deserve, you don't deserve." Feeling guilty
about the past places limitations on us and prevents us
from freely receiving good things in life.

Yes, I did feel somewhat guilty for not practicing what
I preached. It is said that someone once asked Socrates
why he had done a seemingly stupid thing and he
answered that it made sense when he started to do it.
Whatever it is that we did in the past, we did because it
made sense at the time. From the vantage point of the
present, it may appear extremely foolish, but the aim is

to learn from our mistakes and proceed with life, resolving to do better next time. One of our biggest mistakes is to feel unworthy.

It seemed as if the walk home would last forever. There was no hurry as I enjoyed the excitement of the moment. There was peace in my heart, and I knew, as I never knew before, the joy of just being. The sound of footsteps behind me caused me to turn. Approaching was my old friend Gideon wearing a smile as wide as the horizon.

"What are you doing here?" I greeted him as he fell into place beside me.

"It's a beautiful morning and I just wanted to keep you company for a while," he said.

I took it for granted that he wanted to speak with me. "Well," I said, "what good word do you have for me today?"

"First of all, my congratulations on the insights you gained this morning. I had not planned on seeing you for a few days, but the energy generated by your thoughts made me want to rejoice with you. I couldn't wait. You've done extremely well."

"What do you mean?" I asked somewhat startled.

"Walking is a fine exercise, but it's much more than that. Though it benefits you physically, it also has an enormous impact on the mind and spirit. Nature is a great healer and teacher. By being with the trees and clouds, you were able, in your quiet, reflective moments to taste a bit of what we mean by 'oneness with All That

Is.' You have discovered, in a very short time, what you
were trying to recapture and understand for years." He
smiled. "Yesterday, if you recall, you were worried and
concerned about many situations in your life. Our entire
conversation revolved around the unfortunate things
that had happened to you and how you so desired to
improve your lot in life. You were replaying old tapes,
and the sound of the past prevented you from hearing
the music of the present. Your focus was so intense on
making a living that you could not see how to make a life.
Today, that is different."

Although I knew that he was referring to my change of
perception, I still wanted to hear him explain, as if by
listening to his words, I would further confirm what I
already knew. We stopped for a while and sat on a bench
under a large tree. I listened as he continued speaking in
a low voice. "You see, John, when you stopped worrying
about your difficulties, you withdrew your energy from
them. At the same time, you switched your focus to the
things that were going well for you. By doing that, you
changed the way you looked at your world. Whenever
you change the way you look at problems, the problems
themselves start to change."

"But I know all of that, Gideon," I protested. "I am
aware of 'change your thoughts and you change your
world,' and all the rest that goes with it. My question is
why did it take me so long to see things differently?"

"Of course you know," he replied. "Most people know,
but they know in their heads, not their hearts. Knowing

that way is not true knowing. You were only aware of such things. Today, your awareness changed to real knowledge. Again, let me emphasize that awareness comes from the head and knowing comes from the heart. When you really *know* something, you feel it deeply. And as to why it took so long, it is your nature to test various possibilities until you come up with the one that really works for you. Some people do it quickly, others take a little more time."

"All these years, Gideon, I've been living on the outskirts of life, almost like the proverbial prodigal son in a far country. I have been partaking of the crumbs that fall from the table instead of realizing that the table was set for me. Today it is different. I have returned from the far country. I am home."

"But you never were in a far country, John," he answered. "You were always here. Wherever you go, you are always here. All you have to do is realize this and do the best you can with what you have at the time. This is one of the great secrets of life: live joyously in the present moment. As the Zen Master would say, 'When you work, work. When you play, play.' Whatever you are doing, do it with a joyful heart."

It felt so good being there. I stood up and stretched. My entire being seemed filled with a new energy. Gideon sat there observing me with a pleased expression.

"Race you to the house," I yelled at him as I took off. A few minutes later, arriving at my doorstep panting, I looked behind me for Gideon but couldn't see him.

Perhaps he was still sitting on the bench. Then I heard a chuckle, and there on the porch, sitting as calmly as you please, was Gideon holding a rose in his right hand.

"How did you get here before me?" I asked. "I didn't see you pass me."

He smiled as he replied, "There are better ways of getting places than running or rushing. Remember? I was always here. So were you." He stood up, handed me the rose, waved good-bye and left. I stood there watching him as he strode away.

CHAPTER
6

Lighter Than a Feather

Weeks had passed since I had last seen Gideon. I hardly had time to miss him, and besides, I knew that he would soon turn up again. For the moment I was busy employing my new insight. Many were the times during this period when I reasoned that I was going to change my world and myself once and for all. But just as many times, I fell by the wayside. I was either distracted by events that appeared to be overly important or just simply gave up after an initial outburst of enthusiasm.

The secret, it seems, lies in the ability to stick with tasks and see them through despite obstacles. It is also necessary to be kind to oneself. I knew that sooner or later I would encounter a problem that would give me an excellent opportunity to practice what I had learned from Gideon. I was becoming tired of reacting to circumstances instead of responding to them, a subtle but important distinction. React and you are a slave to events and circumstances. Respond and you control them.

It wasn't too long before the opportunity arrived. As a rule, it is not the big test that brings us the most aggravation. It is the accumulation of many small annoyances added together that, most times, makes life miserable. This day, I must have issued an order for all the petty irritations of the universe to report to me for duty. It must have been done at a subconscious level, because I felt I would be a total idiot to consciously desire such a thing.

In any event, I needed to go to the supermarket. Even with the aid of lists and proper planning I found myself visiting the supermarket much more often than necessary. As I pulled into the parking lot, an old pickup truck raced ahead of me and claimed the spot that would have been mine. Nevertheless, I found another spot and parked. I got out, locked the car door and began walking toward the supermarket entrance. A sudden honking and the sound of squealing tires made me jump out of the way of a car that was moving much too fast. To say the least, by this time I was slightly agitated.

Picking up a few items in the supermarket should have been a relatively simple matter. Today it was not. A careless shopper, intent on rushing through the aisles, bumped her shopping cart into mine. This knocked me into a column of stacked cans, causing them to scatter in all directions. Caught off-balance, I slipped and landed on a well-padded part of my anatomy. Looking up, I saw a number of people rushing toward me to see if I needed help. I apologized, picked myself up and walked on as if nothing had happened. I half smiled at the curious onlookers, but inside me was a boiling cauldron.

Finally, at the checkout counter, I felt that I was safe. But even there, I encountered problems. One of the items in my shopping cart did not have a price code. As a result, the entire line was held up while someone was dispatched to find the price. Other impatient customers were glaring at me as if I were totally responsible for their delay. At last, someone found the correct price and I checked out. With a final effort to remain calm, I made my way back to my car, only to find that in my haste I had locked the keys inside.

By this time I had lost all desire to remain calm and controlled. A bumper sticker on the car next to me summarized my true feelings. It said, *Patience, my ass . . . I want to kill somebody.* Placing my bag of groceries on the hood of the car, I wanted to scream. I had a spare key, but it was at home. There must be a better way, I reasoned. And then it struck me. I had been reacting to all the aggravating events that were occurring. All I needed to do was to respond in a more enlightened manner. I had forgotten my resolve to deal with problems on a different level.

How quickly we forget the moments of our glory, the joy of our being. How easy it is for us to become entrapped in the newsreel of life. How natural it seems to react with anger, impatience, hurt and frustration when situations seem beyond our control. This is precisely when we need to realize that we are in the midst of a drama whose script we have written. We are the actor, the director, the playwright, the very play itself. The reasons for our doing this are highly personal and buried deep within us. Even we do not understand why we sometimes test ourselves so sorely.

Once, when I was going through an extremely difficult time, a friend said to me, "It's only a test, John. It will pass."

"Only a test?" I had shouted in anger. "Only a test? I'm tired of being tested! I don't want tests!"

It is necessary to understand that I was not, at the supermarket, faced with problems of major import. There were no life or death decisions to be made. This was just an irritating situation arising out of a number of minor problems. Yet, by my demeanor, one would have guessed that my entire world lay tottering on the brink of annihilation. Seeing this, I decided to handle the situation in a more enlightened manner.

I breathed deeply as I stood there looking at the key in the car. Suddenly I heard the soft voice of a cat. I turned around, and there, staring at me next to the rear door of my car, was the prettiest kitten I had ever seen. It seemed so healthy and well groomed that I was sure it was not a stray. I called to the kitten and it walked over to me. I must return her to her owner, I figured as I picked her up. But there was no one in sight who seemed to have lost a kitten. A deep blanket of calmness was beginning to envelop me as I quietly spoke to the lost kitten. I was now focusing on the kitten's problem instead of mine, and the very shift in thinking made me feel better. However, I was still locked out of my car.

I realized how upset I had been. Those people and events that made me angry were all in the past. It was only my memory of them that was making me miserable. I hardly ever lock my keys in the car. This didn't happen accidentally; there are no accidents. But now I must actively do something. I gently placed the kitten on the hood of the car as I tried the door once more. Nothing happened. I leaned back on the door, closed my eyes for a few seconds and saw myself driving home. Information flashed through my mind. A ridiculous feeling to try the door again. I turned around to look at the kitten, and there she was, quietly staring at me.

I tried the door again, but still no luck. It's a four-door car that I drive. The electric switch locks all the doors at the same time, so it was useless to try the other doors. Nevertheless, I tried them all. It didn't help. I was about to call a cab to take me home for my spare key when the kitten jumped off the hood and ran under the car.

"You'll get yourself killed," I pleaded. "Please come over here."

Quietly she walked back to me. I picked her up and

scolded her, saying, "I've a good mind to lock you in the car until your owner comes," not thinking of what I was saying. At the same time, to show I meant business, I reached over and lifted the handle on the door. There was a click and the door flew open. I just stood there, my jaws as wide open as the door. I had tried that door so many times. I placed the kitten on the back seat while I lifted my bag of groceries from the hood. When I turned around to look, the kitten was gone. I looked all around but could not find her. Perhaps she had gone back to her owner. I breathed a sigh of relief.

Finally, I got in and started the car. What a break, having the door open the way it did. Must have been a defect in the locking mechanism, I surmised. I was ready to pull out when I heard a knock on the window on the passenger side. Before I could see who it was, the door opened and a grinning face peered in.

"May I join you?" he asked matter-of-factly.

"Oh! It's you, Gideon. You should have been here earlier."

Without immediately replying, he slid into the passenger seat and motioned me to drive. As I nudged the car out of the parking space, he asked, "How about my little friend? Wasn't she beautiful?"

"What friend?" I asked.

"The kitten—the one that ran under your car."

"Gideon, were you there all the time? Was that your kitten?"

"No, not my kitten. She's just a friend, who, in her

own way, led you to find a solution to the locked car door."

"Tell me all about it, Gideon. I'm listening."

"Think about it," he replied, "and you'll see how much better and easier it is to solve problems this way. All you have to do is change your mind about the problem. Look at it differently and it will start changing. Whatever you are looking at becomes what you expect."

"There now, Gideon! I did not expect the car door to be locked, but it was, anyway. There goes your theory."

He looked at me the way a good teacher would regard a student who was a slow learner—not in anger or frustration, but with infinite patience. Then he said, "There is a law, a universal law, John, which says that whatsoever you expect out of life, that's what you'll get. When you discovered the kitten, you removed your focus from your problem with the car doors. The problem then resolved itself. That's the secret to solving problems. Remove your focus, your concentration, and the matter is free to fix itself. The result is sometimes astonishing."

I returned to one of my earlier questions, which he had not answered. "Gideon, were you there in the parking lot? Did you have anything to do with all this?"

"No, John," he replied. "I was just an observer this time. The lock was no problem once you realized that you were in control of the situation. I was only watching from a kitten's perspective and enjoying every bit of it, too."

"A kitten's perspective?" I looked at him quizzically.

"Yes, yes," he said. "The kitten. We shared experiences for a short while. Everybody can do that. Just a matter of focus and a little practice."

"Interesting," I replied. "My friend, Gideon, becomes a kitten."

He again gave me that tolerant schoolteacher's look and continued speaking as if he hadn't heard me.

"It's just different life forms working with one another. Love and cooperation. Respect and mutual assistance. Some of the ancient peoples of your earth used that ability constantly. You find it in the legends of those who inhabited this country centuries ago. It exists, to some degree, in the aborigines of Australia. Even in twentieth-century earth there are many who still remember how to do it. Focus and practice, that's all it takes."

"Of what useful purpose is that, Gideon?" I asked.

"Think about it, John. You could exchange information about many things. Learn from one another. Ancient man was able to find food and water with the help of animal friends. Modern man could find peace and joy through such communications. Everything is connected to everything else. Your scientists are just discovering this."

By this time we were approaching my house. I pulled into my driveway thinking that life is, after all, a guided tour of the cosmos. In a little corner of the Universe, I was sitting in my "spacetime" capsule seeing only small parts of the grand design. Somewhere in time I had lost my map and could not even find my tour guide. I turned off the motor as Gideon and I sat for a short while longer.

As if reading my thoughts, he said, "You never lost the map and the tour guide has always been with you. The problem is that in earth life you and millions of others get blinded by appearances. You forget that you are on stage in your own play. You get caught up in your own picture, John. The beginning of your worries is when you feel helpless in your own show. The beginning of your joy and glory is when you realize that all you have to do is change perspective. Practice not to be too attached to your problems. You'll see how soon they'll vanish."

"Gideon, will you come in and meet the children? I know they'll like you."

"Not this time," he replied, "but I'll see them soon."

"When will I see you again? As you can see, there's still a lot for me to learn and you're really an excellent teacher."

"Don't become teacher-dependent, John. You are your own best teacher. Maintain perspective and keep learning. I must go because I promised to have tea with Marla."

"Please say hello for me."

"I will give her your greetings and I'm sure that she would like to see you again. Perhaps we should arrange to get together for dinner one of these days." With this, he opened the door, stepped out and was gone. Yes, life is lighter than a feather, but living is sometimes heavier than a mountain.

CHAPTER
7

Morning Has Been
All Night Coming

It's always engrossing to watch the discovery or rediscovery of a truth. The discoverer is almost always astounded and overwhelmed. It might even appear that the truth was revealed exclusively for his or her benefit. And then, as time moves on, everything returns to its ordinary state again. Yet, once having touched or felt the possibilities beyond the ordinary, one is hardly ever the same as before.

So it was with Gideon and me. A close friendship, an otherworldly comradeship had developed. The things he taught me made sense in my heart but not my head. There were times, however, when darkness closed around and I could make no sense of anything. It was then that I would hear his voice as he quoted a beautiful sentence, "Morning has been all night coming, but see how surely it comes."

It is not the sun that creates darkness, but the earth itself, as it turns its face away from the sun. But the darkness never lasts; the sun is always there and it is we who must return. It is not God who sends us dark times, but we ourselves who bring them to us, for purposes even we do not know. Whenever there are shadows in front of us, it must be that we have our backs to the light. To make the shadows disappear, we have but to turn and face the light.

I have, generally, been given to practicality. A philosophy, a religion, a way of life must be extraordinarily practical to have any effect on me. Don't tell me of a glorious future at the end of this world when I am experiencing difficulty with the present. Let my philosophy and religion show me the way out of darkness into light, and let the way be one that all can walk. Or else, take away your preachings and your pontifications and let me walk my path alone.

As I contemplated these things, I realized how helpful and practical Gideon was. He was trying to show me the way to a more glorious life. His method of teaching was simplicity itself. His was a lifetime of love and understanding, and because I felt his caring, I responded by learning many lessons extremely quickly. He used examples from everyday life and imparted to me not only knowledge, but understanding at the same time.

I remember driving along on a superhighway once, accompanied by Gideon. It was a beautiful day and all seemed peaceful. I was, as usual, questioning Gideon about my concerns. "What is the meaning of life, Gideon?" I asked, more to aggravate him than anything else.

"Life has no meaning, John."

"No meaning, Gideon?" I was shocked.

"Life has no meaning. *You* have meaning. *You* bring meaning to life," he calmly replied.

At about that moment there was the terrifying sound of squealing brakes and honking horns. I reacted quickly as a green sports car cut in front of me without even so much as a signal. It kept weaving in and out, disrupting the synchronized flow of traffic that had existed for the last half hour or so. I was visibly shaken. "That idiot!" I shouted. "He could have caused an accident. Look at him speed, Gideon! He may still cause a wreck."

"He certainly is in a hurry, John," Gideon replied.

"How can you sit there so calmly? The driver almost ran us off the road! We could have had a horrible accident. What do you think about that?"

"'Could haves' don't count. It doesn't matter what could have happened. Only what is happening is important. Listen, calm down and let's keep going. No harm has been done."

These were the times when I wanted, more than anything else, to yell at Gideon or grab him by the neck and squeeze until he abandoned his calmness. How could someone always remain in such control? I knew he had abilities beyond the ordinary, but nevertheless, it was extremely frustrating, and at the same time strangely comforting, to see him responding instead of reacting to circumstances and events.

As if reading my thoughts, he said, "We all must learn sooner or later to respond instead of react. When we react to what seems to be problems, we tend to become reactors and our reaction controls us. When we respond from a higher standpoint of understanding, we then act in a responsible manner and our very response controls circumstances and events. I know that you have given thought to this before."

"It isn't that I don't understand all that, Gideon. It's just so . . . well . . . Actually, you seem so perfect that it makes me think I could not accomplish even a tenth of what you have mastered." I hesitated for a moment and then asked, "Do you see what I mean, Gideon?"

His voice seemed sadder and gentler as he replied, "Do you think I'm able to do these things without ever having to pay a price? Do you think I just woke up one morning, and there I was, with all these abilities and all this wisdom? Do you think it came easy? No, no, my friend. There was a price to pay. I, too, have a 'Gideon' who teaches and helps. He is so far above my level of development that I, too, sometimes despair of ever mastering, as you said, a tenth of what he can. But I keep working. I keep practicing. I keep hoping. And I have the faith that I will get there. And beyond there, too. And you—you are a 'Gideon' to others. Don't you think that, at times, some others look at you and, seeing you as you are, wish they could be heir to some of *your* abilities? Don't you think they, too, become frustrated? On your earth, the growth and learning take time, John. So it's more evolutionary than revolutionary. However, people still search for instant enlightenment.

"Sometimes what is gained in speed is lost in strength. Build strong and at your own pace. Instant gratification is the curse of modern civilization. Yes! Most things require time, John. But then, you have an eternity to do all you would like to do and to accomplish the tasks you have set for yourself. If you combine a measure of knowledge and wisdom with a large dose of practice, you will reach any goal." His voice trailed off as he came to the end. We were both silent for a while.

We had been driving for almost an hour on a trip that normally takes about three hours. The traffic flow had returned to normal. The low hum of the motor and the sound of the wind through the half-open window combined to create an atmosphere of peace.

"Here's a little trick you can use, John." Gideon's voice broke into my thoughts. I glanced at him and was reassured by the half smile on his face. There was a confidence and a self-assuredness about him that always seemed to generate a large degree of comfort within my mind. Gideon continued. "Those who drive cars have a quick way of measuring their awareness level. In fact, by monitoring their driving habits, they can tell whether they are close to center or far out on the circumference of life."

"How so, great teacher?" I asked with tongue in cheek.

"Well, it's really very simple, you see. Not always easy but, nevertheless, very simple. The way you drive is an indication of your level of consciousness. Whenever you find yourself becoming very disturbed by the actions of other drivers around you, look to yourself, for there is an imbalance. You can't do even one little thing to affect the other drivers. You can only be the best driver you possibly can. Don't fret or fume about how others drive. Don't call them idiots or morons. You will cause a rise in your blood pressure and you will be on edge, so that you yourself could precipitate an accident. Don't try to teach people on the highway how to drive.

"Take that driver of half an hour ago. You were disturbed by him. You were angry and rightly so. But don't dwell upon it. It's necessary to let yourself feel. But don't let the feelings of anger, frustration, helplessness, loneliness, despair and others persist for a long time. Natural anger, if handled properly, actually lasts less than a minute. All else that follows is really a reaction to a memory of the event that triggered your anger in the first place.

"What you should have done was gently tap on your brakes as he cut in front of you. Then say to yourself, 'The best place for you is far, far away from me.' And continue driving. In a few moments you would have forgotten the event. You would have remained peaceful, and a peaceful heart is a powerful heart.

"To repeat what I've said, John, when you find yourself becoming upset by other drivers, remember that this is an indication that you need to return to a quiet place in the center of your being. Take it as a road sign. Come back to center. If you practiced enough, you would notice that hardly anything bothers you while you are driving. You would become a much safer driver. You would be protected from accidents, red lights would change to green as you approached them, and parking spaces would open up in crowded parking lots, apparently just for you. There is a practical aspect to all of this, too, you know."

It's always fascinating to me how some people can take the simplest events of life and bring significant meaning to them. Gideon was a master of this art. Whatever circumstances or situations we were experiencing, there always seemed to be a higher meaning for him. And he tried to teach me this. He never grew tired of saying to me, "You never see things as *they* are. You always see them as *you* are. You don't believe what you see, you actually see what you believe."

As I sat contemplating Gideon and his philosophy, that time on the highway seemed far, far away and long, long ago. And yet, I could still close my eyes and in a few seconds call to memory the entire event. The message and the meaning were always there. Would that it were

possible to take all the meanings out of events that occur
and discard the rest. Were it possible not to get caught
up in "what I should have done" or "I wish I hadn't done
that" or, worse yet, "if only," we would be so much
happier, so much more productive, so much more alive.
We tend to live in our yesterdays and fear our tomorrows
and thus miss out on our todays. And each day, I know
a little better, I feel a little stronger, and I understand
with a deeper realization that I am growing into something more glorious, not just going into something more
profitable.

I wished I could see Gideon again, soon. I was also
hoping to see Marla again. How similar was her name to
that of my late wife, Mardai. There is always a curiosity
about our loved ones, to discover where they have gone
and how they are progressing. A strange thought
crossed my mind. Perhaps Marla knew where Mardai
was. Perhaps they could communicate.

My contemplations were interrupted by the ringing of
the phone. I went into the house and picked up the
receiver, only to hear my old friend Gideon's voice.
"John, as I promised the last time I saw you, Marla and
I will be meeting you soon for dinner." Gideon sometimes
got right to the point. No "hello" or "how are you?" No
greeting. Just straight to the point.

"How are you, Gideon? And how is Marla?" I asked.

"We are, as always, fine, John," he answered without
giving me much time to reply. "I know you like bagpipes,
country, classical and many other types of music. We'll

also make arrangements for entertainment at dinner," he continued.

"What are you talking about, Gideon?" I blurted out.

"Dinner, John. You, Marla and I are scheduled for dinner next Wednesday evening at a unique place for a special treat. You'll also get to enjoy some of your favorite music. I'll pick you up at seven P.M. sharp, John. Any problems?"

"Only you," I replied. "You're so confusing."

"I learned that from you, John, and I think sometimes it's rather fun. See you soon."

I hung up the phone. Finally, I'd see Marla again. The full import of the words Gideon had once spoken struck me. Yes, morning does take all night coming, but come, it surely does.

CHAPTER
8

The Restaurant
at the Edge of Eternity

Wednesday, which had seemed such a long way off, finally arrived. The prospect of seeing Marla again was almost unbearably exciting, but deep within me I could still sense a calmness unknown in more ordinary times. I had not seen her in years, but the feeling that she knew something about my wife grew stronger instead of diminishing. Experience foretold that there would be much to learn from dinner this evening. Making the necessary baby-sitting arrangements, I was all dressed and ready before seven.

Gideon was hardly, if ever, late. True to form, at exactly the appointed hour, a long, sleek car pulled into my driveway. A few moments later the doorbell rang and I opened the door to greet Gideon's enigmatic grin. Standing next to him was a picture of great delight and beauty. Marla reached out, shook my hand and gave me a big hug. She seemed not to have aged a day and, if anything, appeared younger and more vivacious than ever.

"Come in please," I said. "Marla, it's so good to see you. I've missed you. Gideon, here, seemed intent on keeping you away from me these many years. Please come in."

"I've been looking forward to our meeting again, John," she proclaimed with a lovely smile.

"We won't come in now; the car is waiting," interjected Gideon. "Let's go, we have a beautiful evening planned."

I went back into the house, kissed the children good-bye and then proceeded out the front door. Gideon, Marla and I walked to the car as a well-dressed chauffeur stepped out and held the door for us.

"What's this with the limo and driver, Gideon?" I asked. "I thought you believed in living simply."

"Living simply is one thing. Living in a miserly condition is another. We should always use the tools at our disposal. So long as a balance is maintained, we can enjoy the gifts we have. Love people and use things instead of using people and loving things. Divine non-attachment, John."

"He always sermonizes like that to me, Marla," I said as we slid into the backseat. The driver closed the door

and we were off. On my right sat my old friend Gideon
and on my left the enchanting Marla.

"Where are we going, Gideon?" I asked.

"To the Restaurant at the Edge of Eternity," he
answered.

"The what at the edge of where?" I blurted out,
somewhat surprised. Marla was the one who answered.

"We figured it would be fun taking a break from your
everyday work, John. That's precisely why Gideon and I
chose this restaurant. It really isn't at the edge of
eternity. Eternity, of course, has no edge—no endings,
no beginnings. It just is. And the restaurant? It's more
than a restaurant. It's a total entertainment system.
Many of our friends visit it on their return from special
assignments. You'll love it, J.H."

"And just where is this restaurant, Marla? Or
shouldn't I ask?"

This time it was Gideon who responded. "You've
traveled with us before, John, so you shouldn't be
surprised that it's not a 'regular' restaurant. Very
shortly we'll experience what is called a 'trans-
dimensional skip,' and before you can blink an eye we'll
be there. No problem. We have reservations, you know."

"I have some reservations, too," I said, not meaning
precisely what he meant.

There are those times when it's useless trying to
obtain more information from Gideon. This was one of
them. I had a feeling of expectancy and a strange sense
of adventure. Gideon, Marla and I had indeed traveled to

many places in different time periods, but that was a long time ago, and I had already forgotten most of it. Yet, here we were again on one of our extraterrestrial or inter-dimensional jaunts. Somehow, my initial uneasiness had begun to dissipate.

It is generally difficult not to be optimistic, happy and peaceful when I am with Gideon. And, with the added enjoyment of Marla's presence, the evening promised to be, in a manner of speaking, "out of this world." I was anxious to ask Marla questions, to learn what she was doing, to know more about her work. When we said good-bye many years ago, I knew I would see her again, but now I wondered if she knew of the trials I had endured since then.

As if in answer to my unspoken questions, Marla said, "Of course I know what you've been going through, John. I don't understand why you insist on using the word 'trials' to describe your journey. Yes, I'm aware of the passing of your wife, the loss of many of those you called friends, the situations where family members turned against you, the perpetual struggle to earn a living for you and your children, and of course, I also know of those lonely moments when you cried out to God for help. At dinner we'll probably touch on some of these matters. Also, you'll probably see some of our old friends, as we told a few folks that we would be there this evening. However, for now, let's just enjoy the ride. We're almost ready for the trans-dimensional shift."

Before I could say anything, the sound of the motor

was replaced by an odd clicking as if someone had suddenly taken possession of the car and were adjusting its instruments. Without warning, there was a dazzling flash of light, and for a moment I felt as if suspended in time and space. I was sure that I was having a lucid dream and that when I woke up, I'd be in my bed. But this wasn't a dream. Gideon made sure I knew that this was real by saying, "You are really experiencing this, John. We'll be there soon."

A few seconds later, or so it seemed, there was a slight bump and the sound of the motor returned to normal. I looked through the window but still could see nothing. Finally we stopped. The driver got out and opened the door, and we slipped out of the car. We were greeted by a young man and a young woman who seemed to have been waiting for us.

"Good evening," the young man said. "This way, please."

We followed the pair into a large, well-lit building, where we were shown to a table. The name card placed on it read, "Gideon and Company."

"What's this with a company, Gideon?" I asked. "Do you own your own company now?"

"No, John, I still work for G&M Enterprises, Inc. This card should have read 'Gideon and Friends.' You remember G&M from the old days, don't you?"

G&M Enterprises was the company for which Gideon and Marla worked when I first met them. The letters stand for God and Man, man being used in the generic sense of the word. The chief executive officer and chairman of the board is God. Many of my earlier learning experiences with Gideon and Marla were staged through adventures with G&M Enterprises.

By this time, we were seated comfortably. Five chairs had been placed around the table. Since there were only three of us, I asked Gideon if we were expecting others to join us for dinner.

"One never knows for sure who will drop in," he said. "I might have mentioned to you before," he continued, "that we oftentimes meet old friends here. This is a favorite 'spacetime' of ours. Marla and I visit very often. The food is excellent and the entertainment is divine." As he said that, a curious smile touched the edges of his mouth.

I had been longing to speak at length with Marla, and now was my opportunity. Before I began, Gideon added, "If you don't mind, John, I'll do the ordering for us. I know exactly what you like."

He busied himself giving instructions to the waiter, and I turned to Marla and asked, "Marla, what do you do these days?" She was a picture of tranquility and understanding. Perhaps I had never noticed before how truly beautiful she was. Her shoulder-length hair seemed to be blowing with the breeze, yet there was no breeze. Slowly she reached over and took my hand in hers. Looking at me with eyes that could illuminate the night sky, she smiled and said, "My responsibilities with the company have increased. I have just completed a major project, and now I've been given possibly the greatest assignment of my career."

"Oh, congratulations!" I exclaimed, feeling her soft warm hands on mine. "Does this mean that we'll see you more often?"

"Well," she said thoughtfully. "My new assignment will certainly make it possible to see you more frequently."

"How so?" I asked.

"John, my new assignment is to assist Gideon in his work with you."

The full impact of her words took a while to sink in. I was becoming uneasy again. Whenever Gideon and Marla had been in touch with me in the past, events seemed to go to extremes. Gideon broke into my thoughts as Marla gently removed her hands from mine to reach for her glass of wine.

"Not to fear, John," he said. "The most difficult part of our work has already been accomplished."

"And what was that, Gideon?"

"It was to stay with you over the past years, but not to interfere in the tests you were going through. Can you imagine how difficult that was for me?"

"No, Gideon! I can't imagine how that could have bothered you. It certainly wasn't a picnic for me. You were watching while I was roasting. Somewhat like Nero fiddling while Rome burned. Why didn't you do something? At least you could have saved Mardai from the illness that took her away. To you it was nothing; to me it was everything. What good is all this stuff and all your power if you don't lift one little finger to help someone, especially one for whom you care?" I was really beginning to uncover old wounds when I realized that I was the guest here and I was behaving in a most improper manner. It was as if I were blaming them for the terrible times of the past. Realizing this, I apologized and continued the conversation.

"I'm sorry, Gideon. I didn't mean to become upset with you. Of course my problems were not your fault. Actually, they were nobody's fault. I guess I'm still a bit sensitive to some of these past events."

"Don't worry about it, John," Gideon replied. "Sometime or the other we must face our dragons and slay them, lest they torture us all our lives."

Marla spoke next. "John, I know that you have many questions for me. I'll give you answers to some of them, even before this evening is done. But others? Well, I must warn you that I don't have all the answers."

I was about to reply when Gideon motioned to my glass of wine. "It's good wine. They bring it in every week from the Aurorian Universal Wine Works . . . somewhere in some remote sector of the galaxy. Try it."

I reached out and picked up the glass. Slowly I raised it to my lips and sipped. I looked at him and nodded. All the while Marla was observing me with amusement in her eyes. I smiled and drank the rest of it.

"Tastes like the proverbial nectar of the gods," I commented.

"Actually, it is," she said.

The lights dimmed for a moment, and Gideon said, "The floor show is about to begin. We'll eat while it's going on."

For the first time I took a good look around the restaurant. It was elegantly decorated. The remarkable thing, however, was its size. Although it seemed as if there were thousands of customers, the hustle and bustle normally present in large restaurants was missing. Everything was flowing so smoothly. In the very center of the room was a large stage that appeared to be simply floating. Inattention on my part or just an optical illusion, I guessed.

Marla's voice brought me back to the dinner table. Standing next to her was a man about six feet tall dressed in a T-shirt and blue jeans. He was whispering to Gideon and must have come to the table while I was glancing around the restaurant.

"John," said Marla, "this is an old friend of ours. Theophilus Marcus. Theo is happy that he could meet you."

We exchanged greetings and he joined us at the table.

"Theo and I have worked on many projects together," Gideon said. "He'll join us for dinner."

"My pleasure," replied Theophilus.

When the waiter brought our dinner, he also brought dinner for Theophilus. Anticipating my question, Gideon said, "Theo passes through here often enough that they know what he likes for dinner. He's a regular."

"I thought you said that the show would start soon, Gideon," I said.

"It has started, John. Each one of us can call up a special show which is exclusively for that person. Others can join in it, if you so desire. There are the controls over there." Gideon pointed to a box with a screen, somewhat like a TV screen. It was controlled by a panel of buttons, each button a different color.

"It's relatively simple to operate, John. I should have explained it to you earlier," Gideon continued. "It's almost like life itself. You press the green button and think about where you want to go and feel how you would like to feel. In an instant you'll be part of the show. If you don't like what you find, or you don't want to stay, just change your mind, strike the red button and everything stops. From that point, you can return to where you started or go directly to another scene. Time and space are no obstruction. It uses that trans-dimensional mechanism I told you about earlier this evening. Very simple gadget, very useful, actually."

"May I try it?" I asked in excitement.

"Whenever you wish," replied Gideon. "Just remember the emergency button in case of problems."

"Problems, Gideon? I thought this was for entertainment. Why would I have problems?" I asked.

Marla jumped in and said, "Life is for entertainment, John, and yet there are problems . . . challenges, if you will. No problems, no growth. No growth, no joy and excitement. No joy and excitement, and one dies of boredom. Better to die of anything than boredom. Then again, one cannot die, but that's another story."

Theophilus, who was sitting quietly all this time, finally spoke. "Gideon, perhaps you or Marla should accompany him this first time. Maybe he would be much more comfortable with someone who knows the system."

"Good idea," said Gideon. "Marla, I will stay and find out what Theo has been up to recently. Why don't you go with John?"

"It would be a delight. Would you like that, John?"

"I'm really not sure what all this means, but I'd love to have you along, Marla," I answered.

Never had I tasted food so delicious. There, in the Restaurant at the Edge of Eternity, I sat with my strange friends enjoying a remarkable meal. It wasn't too long before Marla reached over and whispered, "Whenever you're ready, John. The way it works is simplicity itself. Just think of a place and a time you would like to visit, and when you have the picture clearly in your mind, just press the green button."

"Does it have to be a place I've visited before?"

"No, no. That would be very ordinary; although you could do that, too, if you wanted—just any place and any time. Use your imagination. Close your eyes, if you like. Doesn't matter."

"Just close my eyes and imagine? That's all?"

"When you use your imagination," Gideon replied, "you are using one of the most powerful tools ever given to you by the Creator. Whatever you can imagine, already exists. This mechanism only assists you to find it. Understand that you don't need a machine or tools to do these things. You're perfectly capable of doing anything the machine does. But, since you don't quite know how yet, use the tools."

"OK, Gideon. Let me think of a place and a time. I'll give it a try."

With that I closed my eyes and, at the same time, made sure that my finger was resting lightly on the green button. I didn't want any mistakes. Marla's hand felt comforting on mine as I took a deep breath and let my mind wander.

CHAPTER
9

Will Ye No Come Back Again?

There is a village in Scotland far from the bustling of busy cities. Or at least there was. Go, as the crow flies, north from Cromarty, beyond Dornoch Firth, toward the Northwest Highlands, and you will cross green, gently rising countryside and see the hills and lochs of this ancient land. You cannot help but be caught up in a spirit of exhilaration and freedom. Before you reach the ocean, about fifty miles away, turn sharply to your right and proceed directly east toward the North Sea. If you carefully follow my directions, you will come upon a little village nestled in the arms of the beautiful hills of Forever and kissed by the waters of Eternity.

I have never seen this village, and yet, I know it's there. Perhaps Mardai's great-grandfather roamed the highlands and visited that village. He was Scottish, you see. As a young lad, I remember the rapture I felt at the sound of the bagpipe. I loved just to stand and listen to a lone piper, piping away at eventide. The bagpipe fascinates me even to this day, so much so that I follow the Scottish festivals and literally spend hours treading behind the pipers. I see myself taking the high road and following the low road beyond Loch Lomond until I meet that special someone coming through the Rye. Then off I go singing the Skye Boat Song to where the River Afton flows gently through County Ayrshire. The land of Robert the Bruce and Mary Queen of Scots holds a very special fascination for me.

Suddenly, my mind returned to the Restaurant at the Edge of Eternity, to Marla, Gideon and Theo. I opened my eyes and with firm resolve said to Marla, "I have always wanted to visit Scotland and to go alone the first time. Do you mind, Marla?"

"No, John. I quite understand." A shadow of sadness crossed her face. Perhaps it was my imagination. However, the pull of that little village was so strong and I felt the need to be alone.

"I can't explain it, Marla. I just must be alone with my thoughts."

"There are times we all need 'aloneness.' Here, clip this remote control to your belt. The buttons on the main panel are duplicated on the remote. Remember, green for go, red to stop or to change programs. The white button is for me. If you change your mind about being alone, press the white button. I will come. There is also a small instruction sheet pasted on the back of the remote control in case you forget what to do or need further instructions."

"You are sure this thing is safe, aren't you?" I asked, more to hear myself say it than to be reassured.

"Always safe, John" was her reply. "Anything else is just an appearance based on your belief. Never forget that."

She leaned closer to me and kissed me on the cheek. Gideon and Theo sat quietly looking on. I closed my eyes again. This time I could see the village clearly. I knew I had to go there. A shrill sound broke into my stillness. The sound of a bagpipe, it seemed so near and, yet, so far away. Gently, ever so gently, I pressed the green button.

The music seemed to come closer. Nothing else happened. I gradually opened my eyes. The restaurant, Marla, Gideon and everything else were gone. I was sitting under a large oak tree. Standing not fifty paces away was a lone piper playing away as the sun began to set. The mournful tune rang out across the hills and woods, and I knew I was visiting an ancient home.

The peace surrounding me at that instant was indescribable. I soaked up every variation of the music into the very cells of my body. Time seemed to stand still, caught between a curious traveler and a Scottish village of long ago. The music came to an end, but I just sat there, motionless for a while longer.

The piper looked at me, smiled and said, "They'll be expecting you soon. Let's go." And he turned and piped as he slowly marched back to the village. I followed him at a distance until, over the next hill, I saw the village fires. A group of people were standing by in tense anticipation. As soon as they caught sight of me, they rushed over. By this time, the piping had ceased.

"You found him, eh, Charlie?" one of the group asked the piper. I gazed about, quietly taking in the scene. One part of me was so much at ease that I felt I belonged there. Another part felt as if I were watching an old movie replay itself gently across the screen of my mind.

"Yes. At the right time and place. Just as we were told" was Charlie's reply.

For the first time since arriving here I spoke, addressing Charlie directly. "Charlie, that music was wonderful. Who is in charge here?"

An elderly couple stepped out of the small crowd, and both bowed low as the man spoke.

"My chieftain! Welcome back. My wife and I are in charge now. We knew you'd come again. You'll stay with us tonight, I hope."

I wondered why he addressed me as "My chieftain" but thought it must be an old Scottish custom. It was almost as if I'd done this before.

"There seems to be somewhat of an emergency here," I said. "Why are you so worried, Donald?" I knew his name without even knowing how.

"My lord," he answered. "There's a child in the village who is very ill. You are here to make him well."

"I am? . . . Oh, of course, I am," I said, somewhat surprised but not wanting to show my ignorance.

I wasn't really sure why I seemed to remember giving some medicine to a sick child in this village, but I wasn't worried about it. The old man led me to a house on the other side of the village. The others followed slowly. Entering the house, I was led to a boy lying on a bed covered with thick quilts. A woman, who I guessed was his mother, sat on an old wooden chair next to him holding his hand lovingly. Donald remained in the background as I walked up to her. She rose from her chair, grasped my hand with tears in her eyes and said, "You must help him, sir. The fever is very high."

"Alex will be fine in the morning," I said, trying to comfort her. Again, I knew his name without really understanding how I knew.

"Oh, thank you, good sir. God bless you."

"God blesses all of us," I replied. Turning to Alex, I continued, "You will sleep well this evening, Alex. The fever will go away tonight. I've brought you something." I felt somewhat awkward as, for some unexplained reason, I reached into my pocket and pulled out a small bottle. It was one of those little pharmacy prescription containers. I didn't remember bringing it, but I still seemed to know that it was there. I emptied two of the little white pills into the palm of my hand.

I handed them to Alex's mother, saying, "Give these to him with a glass of water. Here are the rest. Make sure he takes them, two at a time, three times a day, until they're all gone. He'll regain his strength very soon."

She followed my instructions, and finally, Alex was sleeping peacefully. I then turned to Donald and said, "My work here is done. I will stay until the morning, if you don't mind."

He led me away from Alex's house to his own house, overlooking the sea. There was excitement in his voice as he said, "My chieftain, please stay until tomorrow. The rest will do you good. Your quarters are already prepared."

"I think I'd like that, Donald. Are you sure it's no trouble?"

"No trouble, I assure you. All the villagers, including myself, will forget about tonight. That is how it is supposed to work. But little Alex—little Alex will remember, and as he grows older, it will seem as a dream to him."

"Who is Alex, anyway?" I asked. "I thought I knew him or had seen him someplace before."

We stood there on the porch, this old man and I. He looked at me with the wisdom of the ages in his eyes as he calmly said, "Alex is the one who will, in years to come, make a discovery that will bring him fame. He'll change the course of medicine by giving the world what will come to be known as penicillin. That little boy, my lord, will one day be known as Sir Alexander Fleming. He will go on to become a winner of the Nobel Prize in medicine."

I stood there, dumbfounded. Although I knew that I had wanted to come to this little village, I'd thought it was only for entertainment. I could hardly believe that there was another purpose, yet it felt so good to have been able to give Alex some much-needed medication.

"Those pills," continued Donald, "are penicillin tablets you brought with you to help heal the person who would eventually discover penicillin."

"Isn't it strange, Donald? Isn't it weird that I brought the substance he is going to discover, so that he may live to discover it?"

"Not strange at all, my chieftain," replied Donald. "Not strange if you realize that we can change our future by working with the past. Or affect our past by working in the present, and thereby create a whole new future. Pasts, presents and futures are all constructs of the human mind while in the physical body."

"How do you know so much, Don? And why do you insist on calling me 'chieftain'?" I asked.

"To answer the second part of your question first, sir, you *are* my chieftain. We have worked together before. You helped me so much in my spiritual growth that I will always be grateful to you. We belong to the same family, if I may be so bold. I chose to stay in this little village and give my gifts here. Most of the other villagers do not know this. Charlie the piper knows, and so does Duncan. My current earth job is to build villages, to help ordinary people with their everyday problems, to, every once in a while, assist in the production of a Sir Alexander Fleming and, hopefully, to grow and reach toward the stars at the same time.

"You see, my chieftain, you have always helped me to help others. Like me, you, too, do not remember the things you do in other dimensions. You may not remember the time we gathered together from all parts of the earth, a hundred thousand bright, shining lights. It was a time of great turmoil and there were wars and rumors of wars. We came together and spoke of love and compassion. There, you taught some of us about the love our Creator has for us and how our joy in life would spring from giving service to others. You showed us by example that we were all shining lights and that, to shine brighter, we were to always lend a helping hand to our less fortunate brothers and sisters.

"You explained to us the sacred nature of all life forms, and you taught us to respect their unique lives. We watched you as you went through your very own trials and tribulations and saw you in agony as you yearned for peace and joy. But never did we see you lose hope. Never, never did we hear you cry out and curse your God. Though you fell, you got up. When the rivers of faith almost ran dry, you still maintained hope. Although our hearts ached for you, you were and always will be our inspiration. So, you see, you are my chieftain. As for the first part of your question, I know so much because you taught me so much."

We were both quiet for a while. The sound of the waves on the shoreline of the village was soothing music to my ears. A northeasterly wind began blowing and gently caressed my face as it warmed my body and soul.

Donald stood next to me and, from the corner of my eye, did not appear as old and weathered as when I first saw him. A strong bond was developing between us. The Scotsman and I stood there enjoying the contemplation of just being, of just living, of life itself.

"Wasn't Fleming born in Lochfield?" I asked. "What's he doing here?"

"Yes, that's true, but he was visiting. He'll return soon, and then he'll start the work that will lead to his greatest contributions to humanity."

"A little later I might go for a walk on the beach, Donald," I said. "It's a clear evening and so comfortably warm. Look," I continued, pointing upward, "there is Orion, the Hunter, and his dog. I feel the call of those stars."

"I won't accompany you on your walk," said Donald. "However, why don't we have dinner first and then the rest of the evening will be yours. Charlie would be delighted to have you join us for dinner at his home. He's preparing a real Scottish dinner. You know, he lives alone now. After his wife died a few years ago, he never remarried. He doesn't have any children or kin in these parts, but he so enjoys bringing pleasure to everyone with his bagpipe. I'm sure he'll play for you, if you come."

"Dinner and the bagpipe, too? Why, of course, Donald. How could I refuse? When do we go?"

"Now, if you like," he responded.

"Good, let's go have a great time at Charlie's place."

As we approached Charlie's house, a melancholy refrain floated down to greet us. We walked up to his door and knocked; interrupting his music, Charlie ushered us inside.

"I'm so glad you could come," he said. "I know how busy you are, but we don't get to see you much these days. How are Gideon and Marla?"

"Do you know them?" I asked, surprised.

"Of course, my lord. They stop by every now and then. We are truly honored when they visit. Please tell them to come again, soon."

"I certainly will tell them. And please, Charlie, you and Donald stop calling me 'my lord' and 'my chieftain.' It's rather disconcerting."

"Very well, my lord," Donald replied. "But we've grown accustomed to addressing you this way. It'll take some getting used to."

We enjoyed a hearty meal. Charlie was as good at cooking as he was at piping. Dinner over, we relaxed to those lovely tunes, which to me are such a delight. Finally, I looked at my watch and saw that it was 10:30 P.M. That was when I realized that I had my remote control clipped to my belt and that I was dressed quite differently from the people of this time and place. Yet, no one seemed to have noticed. I leaned back, closed my eyes for a second and thought I heard Marla's voice say, "It's okay, John. They see you as they are. Don't worry." For a moment I'd almost forgotten where I was. This trans-dimensional travel could be tricky, indeed.

"I must go now, my dear friends," I said to Donald and Charlie. "I still want to take that walk along the beach. I know how to find my way around, so, Donald, you can stay and visit a bit longer with Charlie, if you like."

"I'll do that," said Donald.

"Will I see you in the morning before I leave?" I asked.

"If that is your wish" was his reply. "Have yourself a very good night."

I left them standing there and walked slowly toward the sound of the ocean. The music of the bagpipe was lost in the sound of the wind and the breakers as I stepped into a breathtaking moonlit scene. There by the sea, I sat down under a giant tree and gazed up at the pale moon and the starry heavens. "This is so beautiful, so peaceful," I said to myself. "Beautiful and peaceful things should be shared with others."

CHAPTER
10

Things That Go Bump
in the Night

The wind in the leaves above reminded me of poems I'd read about mystical lands and climes, though where I was tonight was mystical in itself. Thoughts flooded my mind, tumbling over one another in an effort to grab my attention. I had concentrated my focus so intently into the present that I could scarcely remember I was supposed to be having dinner with Gideon and Marla. Time often appears to be relative, resembling situations in everyday life when whatever it is that you are doing is enjoyable and full of excitement. It seems to speed up or slow down, even stand still, while we immerse ourselves in the matters of the moment.

My mind returned to dinner, and then to my children, my home and my work, and I began to feel uneasy. Tomorrow would be a new day with new challenges, and here I was whiling away the hours with restaurants, bagpipes and trans-dimensional shifts. For all I knew, this was a dream, and everyone knows that strange things can happen in dreams. Perhaps there was no such thing as a trans-dimensional shift or no such place as a Restaurant at the Edge of Eternity. What was I doing here? I felt I must return to wherever I had come from, or, at least, I must wake up from this dream.

Anxiety was beginning to overwhelm me when I suddenly remembered the remote control on my belt. I hurriedly got up, grasped it and stared at the buttons. "Press red," Gideon had said, "if you want to stop or change the program." And the white button was to call Marla. By this time, my palms were wet with perspiration. No longer could I hear the ocean or see the moon above. My thoughts continued racing faster and faster. What had started out as a beautiful fantasy evening was fast becoming a horrible nightmare.

I reached toward the red button and stopped just a fraction of an inch away. "Perhaps not the red," I thought. "Perhaps the white first. Let's see what happens with the white. Press the white button. Go on, John, push the white button . . . Now." With great effort, I moved my finger to the white button. The entire scene appeared to be in slow motion. I was reminded of those TV movies where the hero is moving away from the scene of the crime. The faster he tries to move, the more obstacles appear to block his way. My finger finally reached the white button and I pressed. It clicked easily, and I stood there, as if suspended, waiting for something to happen.

At first, nothing seemed to happen, and then, out of the moonlight, from the beach, came a sound. It was as if someone were calling my name. I leaned forward to see a little better and noticed a figure in a white, flowing dress walking toward me. There was a familiarity in that walk—long, graceful and purposeful. And then I heard Marla's voice again above the wind and the sea.

"John," she said. "You called. Here I am."

By this time she had reached where I was standing and, with both arms extended, enveloped me in a big hug.

"Marla," I exclaimed, "I was beginning to become frightened by what was happening. I was starting to think that this was all make-believe and that I had no right to be here and I was not supposed to—"

"Hold it, John," she interrupted. "I know. That's precisely the reason I wanted you to have access to the white button on your control. I had a feeling you would need me."

"I'm sorry," I replied, somewhat dejected. "I didn't mean to cause any trouble. It was just that . . . it was, well . . ."

"No need for explanations," she said. And then she added, "It's a beautiful night. Let's walk down by the water. Or would you prefer to return to the restaurant now?"

"I promised that I would stay until morning, because of those two chaps, Donald and Charlie. By the way, Donald said he knows you and Gideon."

"All of us know one another, John. Everything is connected to everything else. Those of us who have the same goals, the same loves, similar hopes and dreams, those of us who are from the same 'family,' meet often enough to know one another fairly well."

"If I were to stay here until morning, what would happen when I return to the restaurant? I mean, would Gideon and Theo be gone? And my children? I didn't tell them and the baby-sitter that I would be away all night."

"You still worry about so many matters, my friend." Marla spoke softly and with understanding. "There is no problem with whatever time you choose, because no time will have passed when you return. You've done this before with Gideon, but you've probably forgotten."

"I still don't understand these things too well. Okay. I guess I'll stay here tonight. Tell me, though, why did I start worrying so much when I was sitting under that tree?"

By this time we had reached the edge of the water. We continued walking along the shore for a while before Marla answered.

"Being here is no different from being anywhere else, John. You're subject to the same thoughts and feelings wherever and whenever you go. True, there are some places that amplify certain situations and others that diminish them. But in general, you're always in control of your thoughts and your feelings. At first you were fine, handling events in a first-rate manner. Then you went for a walk and finally sat under a tree to reflect on your thoughts and to enjoy the evening.

"Initially, it was nothing but a stray thought that entered your mind. That was easy because you ignored it. Then another thought, and this time you looked at it a bit more carefully, if you see what I mean. Finally you began to consider various possibilities, and as you did that an old acquaintance of yours reared its ugly head. It was that tyrant whom you call 'doubt.' It came into your mind and would have passed through unnoticed had you not asked it to remain and keep you company.

"Now, I do not mean that literally. I just mean that you let your doubts run away with you. You forgot the times of your triumphs and successes. You ignored the fact that you had just enjoyed a most magnificent evening, complete with bagpipes and even time travel. You gave in to your doubts about who you are and what you were doing here. The second you did that, you opened the door for fear. As fear entered, your perspective altered. Pay particular attention to the fact that nothing changed except the way you looked at things. As your perception changed, your entire world seemed to change also.

"Notice how the moon seemed to disappear and you ceased hearing the sound of the sea. That's when you reached for the white button."

"You know that I did all those things, Marla?" I asked.

"Of course, I knew. We were monitoring you closely. No harm could have come to you, but we were concerned about your working yourself into an emotional lather, which would have made you totally miserable. So, I'm glad you called me and I'm happy I could come to assist you."

"There's meaning to everything, right, Marla?"

"Yes. There are a few exceptions, but they are extremely rare. Generally, there's a purpose for everything," she answered.

"Well, tell me, what was the lesson in all I just went through?"

"Simple. Believe in who you are. Have faith in yourself and your God. Trust the guidance within you. Do not give way to doubt and fear. Nothing complex at all."

"It seems so easy, now that you've explained it."

"Another problem people have," Marla continued, "is that they refuse to ask for help, even when they know that assistance is waiting for them. Some foolish pride or misguided concept of independence prevents them from asking. You have that problem, too, John, but this time you asked. You finally called me."

"Yes, I remember now. Help is always there for us. We were not thrown into the cosmos as biological accidents. We're children of our Creator with the power to alter creation itself. Yes, I know all these things, but sometimes I, too, become anxious and forget."

"It's easy to forget who you are. Fear, frustration, anger, doubt, greed, selfishness . . . these are the reasons for forgetting. Love, peace, joy, quietness, compassion, aloneness . . . these help you to remember; these help to reinforce your oneness with God and validate your existence and worth. People are so busy trying to make a living that they have no time to make a life."

We had been walking all this time. The tranquility and confidence of hours before had now returned. We stopped for a while to breathe in the freshness of the ocean air. The moon was full once again, and the roar of the waves joined with the rustling of the leaves to create a symphony more hypnotic than the mythical song of Ulysses' sirens.

We reversed our direction, back to where I was sitting when Marla first arrived. I reflected on what an evening it had been, as I glanced at Marla. How different were our worlds, I thought. How perfect or so near to perfection she was, a radiant mind and spirit in an alluring body. The moonlight bouncing off her flowing golden hair created myriad dancing stars around her head. It took little to imagine one could easily fall in love with such a vision.

We had been quiet for some time, just enjoying the sights and sounds around us, so that Marla's voice startled me when she spoke. "I never could understand why human beings always 'fall' in love. How much better it would be if they would only 'rise' in love."

"There you go reading my thoughts again, Marla," I said with some embarrassment.

"I never do that. It's not permitted to violate the privacy of others. Only under certain emergency conditions, and then only for their benefit, is it ever done," she replied.

"Then how come you knew what I was thinking?" I asked.

"Our thoughts became one for a little while, so I was aware of the essence of what was in your mind. You do that all the time, you know. How often in the past few years have you been able to answer people's questions before the questions were even asked?"

"Yes, I see what you mean," I said. Now I was thinking of Mardai and the years we had spent together. Memories of the past started flowing fast and furious through my mind. But this time I wasn't going to be overcome by emotions. I was going to come over them, instead.

"Marla, I have always felt that you knew my wife. There seems to be a connection between the two of you."

"Yes, I know her. We know each other fairly well."

"Do you know where she is now? How is she and what is she doing?" My words were tumbling out so fast that Marla had to slow me down.

"Easy, John, one thing at a time." She paused for a while then continued. "She and I, as well as others, have been together from the beginning, if you insist on 'sequential' time. If you prefer to think in 'simultaneous' time, then we are always together."

"Please, Marla, don't make it too complex. Just tell me where she is and what she's doing."

"There isn't much to tell. Her work with you here on the physical earth plane was done. Had she stayed any longer, you might not have gone on to finish the job you came here to do. She felt she could do no more to help you with your work, and so she went on ahead, knowing that when you had completed the tasks you set yourself, you would join her.

"She is always near you, and even this very evening as you sat under the old tree, her presence was with you. A love that is born of eternity lasts throughout eternity. The only reality in heaven or earth, the only thing that counts, is how deep and true our love is. Her love for you has always been true and steadfast. She helps you in your work and in your everyday life. She watches over the children and assists in their development. She is as much a part of your life now as she ever was. The only difference is that the physical presence is gone; however, the spiritual body can never die. You never lost her. Love never loses. You and Mardai are bound together by ties that span the universe itself.

"Continue your work. It will make you happy. It will make her happy also. You have a few good friends, your children, your health, your sense of purpose. You've gathered considerable wisdom on your journey. Use it well. Gideon and I are here to help you. Call us when you need us. Mardai understands, better than you think, the situations in which you find yourself. She hears you when you speak to her. She also answers your questions and often speaks to you, but you do not hear her clearly yet. Keep practicing."

Marla became silent. We had covered substantial territory in our conversation. I knew the time was fast approaching when she would return to the friends she had left at the restaurant. I was, however, no longer worried, fearful or frustrated.

"I guess you're planning to leave now," I said.

"Unless you need me to stay longer."

"No. I'll see you again soon, anyway."

"Then I'll be going," she said. "There's a lot you have to think about." She hugged me tightly and smiled. We stood there for a moment longer before I turned and walked back to Donald's house. When I glanced back, Marla had vanished.

I tiptoed into the house so as not to wake my sleeping host. By this time, I was tired. It had been an adventurous evening, full of entertainment and learning. We are truly our own best friends, but there are those times when we can, as well, be our own greatest enemies. A short while later I drifted off to sleep.

The next morning, I thanked Charlie and Donald for their warm hospitality. We spoke for a while about their hopes for the village, and I promised to visit them again one day. I was going to miss these two. Sadly, I said good-bye, then pressed the red button on my remote control while picturing Gideon, Marla and Theo in my mind's eye. Within a few seconds I was back, seated next to them at the restaurant. They appeared to be in the middle of the same conversation as when I left.

"Welcome back, John," said Gideon. "I know you had an excellent trip. Welcome back."

CHAPTER
11

A Dream Is a Dream Is a . . .

While I had been gone, time seemed to have stood still. I had heard about such things before and had even experienced some of them once or twice, but whenever it's happening again, it's almost always new and exciting. Before I could say anything to Gideon, Theo asked, "Would you like some dessert, John?"

"No, thank you," I replied. "I have quite enough food for thought."

"Yes, I understand," he said. "Sometimes people spend so much time on food for the body that they neglect feeding the mind and spirit."

"Well," I replied, not knowing what else to say, "it was

certainly an interesting evening. I think I would just like to go home now."

Gideon asked, "Are you feeling tired?"

"Not tired, Gideon. I just want to get away from this otherworldly stuff for a while. Too much of it can give a person mental indigestion, you know. Perhaps I'm not yet ready for all this. Tomorrow, I have to be back in the regular, everyday world, answering telephones, working, taking care of children, paying bills and—"

Gideon interrupted, "Now, now, let's not get into that again. You speak of working and all the other tasks you face as if they were horrible matters to be avoided at all cost. I've told you before that when your work becomes enjoyable, when you're doing the things you most want to do, when you're serving others instead of self, then the rewards are overwhelming. Give service and you give of yourself. Give of yourself and the return is assured."

"Fine, Gideon," I replied. "I'll try to be more understanding of myself and others. I'll try to keep perspective in everything." I was hoping to change the direction of his conversation without appearing rude, but he would not let me off so easily.

"John," he said rather intensely, "don't talk about 'trying.' 'Try' is one of the most negative words in your language. Whenever someone says that he is trying, it means that there isn't a real commitment. If you speak or think 'try,' the subconscious knows you're not serious. Don't 'try,' just 'do' or . . . don't 'do.'"

"Thanks, Gideon," I said, somewhat apologetic for forgetting the things I knew.

"You're welcome, John" was his response. "Look at Theo here. He's been having a tough time, and yet, he keeps working against tremendous odds. Still, I know he enjoys doing what he does."

"What do you do, Theo?" I asked.

Theo took a deep breath, looked at me and replied, "I am into trees, John."

"Into trees?" I asked with a foolish expression on my face. "Into trees? Exactly how do you do that?"

"Don't look so surprised," said Theo. "Let me explain. Your primary source of food on earth is from those factories you call 'trees.' For centuries people have been systematically destroying vegetation on earth. The situation has become critical. Your rain forests are being destroyed, your rivers have become polluted, and in some areas, you can't breathe the air. People think that it is someone else's problem, but let me assure you, it is everybody's duty to do something about it. If the condition is not reversed soon, your children and your children's children will suffer. My assignment is to help stop the environmental destruction of your planet. There are a number of us working on this. Sometimes it seems hopeless, but we'll continue our work. We're seeing some signs of change, few though they be."

"What can I do to help?"

"Quite a lot, actually," he said. "You and your children

can plant some trees in your yard, and take better care
of the ones you now have. If everyone did that, you
would see remarkable changes. There are many groups
who are trying to save the environment. Support some of
them. Carefully choose the products you use in your
home. Paper comes from trees. Support companies that
use recycled paper. Deliver your old newspapers to a
recycling unit. It may take a few more minutes of your
time, but it will help considerably. Each person can do
small things to help. And a lot of small things add up to
big results."

Here I was, concerned about the major problems I
faced in life, and there was Theo telling me about trees.
Yet, what he said truly made sense. Sometimes we are
so busy with the things that seem important that we
forget those that are truly of importance—our children,
our mates, our friends, our earth.

"I think I'll have some more wine," I said as I reached
for the bottle. I poured some in my glass and offered
some to the others. It certainly was the best wine I had
ever tasted.

"Some of my radical religious friends tell me that I'll go
to hell for drinking this stuff, Gideon." I was just
commenting without expecting a reply, but Gideon ex-
pressed his views, anyway.

"Remember Jesus?" he asked. "He enjoyed wine. His
very first miracle, as recorded in the narrative, was
turning water into wine. He was quite a favored dinner

guest in Jerusalem, you know. The key is moderation in all things, John. Too much of anything will create imbalances. Enjoy the wine, don't overdo it, don't analyze it."

"Now that you've brought up Jesus, remember you, me and Marla at that party years ago? I'd like to do that again. What do you think?" I asked. "Would that be possible?"

"It was a great get-together," said Marla, "but it was also a different spacetime situation. You learned so much from the experience that you were able to go through some of the most difficult years of your life without giving up. What did you enjoy most when you were there, John?"

I noticed that she hadn't answered my question but had asked me one instead. Neither Marla nor Gideon ever used idle words. Everything they said had some deeper meaning. Every question asked had significance.

"I'm really not sure whether it was a dream or it actually occurred, Marla. It's been such a long time. I guess it's not really important anyway." I said all that without really giving much thought to what I was saying.

"Come now, John!" Marla said. "You meet with God and it's not important? You ask questions of Jesus, the Buddha, Gandhi and others, and you wonder whether you were dreaming or really experiencing the events? You conversed with your dad who had died a few years earlier, and you think it's your imagination? Listen,

John, there is an extremely fine line between reality and dreams. In their own dimensions, they are each very real. The trick is to know which is which and to put to use the information you get from both."

"Well, I'm sorry if I seem so hardheaded, Marla," I retorted. "There are times when life can be extremely perplexing. One day you're up and everything appears perfect. The next day you're down and the whole world seems to be turning against you. I'd really like for God to explain to me in a few simple sentences how to make life work. Could we arrange for another meeting so that, once and for all, my questions will be answered?"

It was Gideon who answered this time. "We could arrange for you to meet with the personalities you referred to. But remember, they cannot change your life. Only you can do that. Whatever else you want to say about life, one thing is certain, *life is*, it just is. Not death and taxes. Just life and the universe."

"I seem to be a poor dinner guest this evening, my friends," I said. "Perhaps it's just because I'm tired and need some rest. Can we go now? We'll speak about these things some other time."

Theo got up, wished us all a fine evening, said goodbye and left Gideon, Marla and me sitting there.

"Yes, it's about time you get back," Marla said as we prepared to leave.

"Thanks for such a great evening," I said. "I wish that I had been better company."

"John, stop putting yourself down. There has been

enough of that in the past. We enjoyed your company. You're just striving to learn more, to know more and to be a better person. That's why you ask so many questions. You can never annoy us. We love you too much. Let's go. After you get a good night's rest, you'll feel much better."

"Thanks, Gideon. Please, let me help pay for dinner."

"No, John. It goes on my expense account. Remember we work for G&M Enterprises, Inc. The pay is first-rate and the benefits package is excellent."

"Why don't you get me a job with your company, Gideon?" I asked. "I could certainly use some of those benefits and I'm sure I'd enjoy the increase in pay."

There was that twinkle in his eye again as he replied, "You already work for the company, John. In fact, you, Marla and I are in the same department. Your problem is you think that you're working for everyone else, even though you work only for yourself and the company."

"What do you mean?" I asked, but he did not explain any further.

By this time we had arrived at the front of the building. The same limousine was parked, ready to pick us up. As we got in, Marla leaned over and whispered, "It was a very pleasant evening. We'll see you again, soon."

The doors closed and I heard the ringing of a telephone. Why would anyone be calling now? I was feeling extremely drowsy and my eyes must have closed for a second. The ringing of the phone continued and I jumped up. To my surprise, I found myself in my bed at home, and the ringing was coming from the phone on the bedside table. I reached over and grabbed it, not knowing for sure where I was or what was going on.

"Hello," I said, glancing at the clock; it read 7:11. It was morning time. "Hello," I said again.

The voice on the other end answered, "It's your wake-up call, Mr. H. Have a pleasant day!"

Before I could say anything further, there was a click as the caller hung up. I replaced the receiver and sat up in bed to clear my mind. I don't get wake-up calls at home. I had to sort things out. How did I get here? I remembered leaving for dinner last night with Marla and Gideon and making arrangements for baby-sitting. The restaurant, Theo, Marla and Gideon were fresh in my mind. The little Scottish village by the sea, the bagpipes, Charlie and Donald. To say the least, I was bewildered and a bit disoriented.

In the middle of trying to put the pieces together, there was a banging on my bedroom door, and as they sometimes do, Malika and Jonathan rushed in.

"Hi, Daddy!" shouted Jonathan.

"We thought you were sleeping," said Malika. "But when we heard the phone, we knew you had to be awake."

"Hi, kids," I said. "Is everything OK?"

They must have seen the consternation in my face as I

sat there. Malika replied, "Yes, of course. What's the matter, Daddy?"

"Nothing. Did you and Jonathan have a good time last evening? You didn't give the baby-sitter a rough time, I hope."

"Baby-sitter?" she asked. "What baby-sitter?"

"The one who took care of you last night," I said. "What do you think I'm talking about?"

"We didn't have a baby-sitter last night, Daddy. Are you sure you're OK?"

"Maybe you were just dreaming and the phone woke you up in the middle of your dream," said Jonathan.

I looked at them curiously and then said, "Yes, I must have been dreaming. It seemed so real."

"Tell us about your dream, Daddy," said Malika.

Not wanting to say much, I replied, "It was something about going out to dinner with friends and leaving you and Jonathan with a sitter. That's how dreams are, you know. They seem so real."

"You were so tired when you came home from the office yesterday," Malika said, "that immediately after dinner, you told us you needed a nap. You changed into your nightclothes and fell asleep. It was very early. You really slept for a long time. I hope you're rested now and feel a lot better."

"And, Daddy," said Jonathan, "you left the lights on. Malika and I turned them off."

"Well, thank you. Let's go get washed up and I'll be down for breakfast in a few minutes," I said.

I got out of bed and after a little while went downstairs for breakfast. Saturdays and Sundays have always been very special days for me and the children. During the week, they attend school and I go to the office. But on weekends we spend as much time as possible with one another. They grow so quickly and then they're gone. I wanted to enjoy every moment I spent with them. Although it may appear at times that raising children is 90 percent sheer frustration and 10 percent pure enjoyment, I think the joy, and the love, make it all worthwhile. Like most other Saturdays, today promised to be fun.

After breakfast, the children wanted to go over to a friend's house for a short while. When they were gone, I went upstairs and decided to rearrange some of my books while listening to music. Last night's dream was still so vivid. If I listened carefully, I could still hear the mournful sound of bagpipes and the crash of the ocean upon the shores of the little village.

Thinking about nothing in particular and everything in general, I was starting to put the dream into the background of my mind when I noticed a sheet of paper at the foot of my bed. Paper comes from trees, I mused as I reached down and picked it up. Trees? Theo was speaking about trees last evening. Who was Theo? Oh, the dream, of course. Well, dreams are dreams and reality is reality, and though they are two distinct segments of life . . . thus ran my thoughts.

I glanced at the writing on the sheet of paper, assuming that it belonged to Jonathan or Malika. There, penned in beautiful letters, were the words, "Dinner at the Restaurant at the Edge of Eternity—7:00 P.M." I stared at it again, as I stood there in total amazement. Perhaps my dream was not a dream after all.

CHAPTER
12

This, Too, Shall Pass

Days passed without any sign or communication from Gideon or Marla. Although this was not unusual, I wanted so badly to discuss my dream with them. Was it really a dream? And if it was not, then what had happened? The normal chores of everyday life took over again, and I busied myself with meeting the ordinary problems at hand. Deadlines seemed to be everywhere. I never did like the word "deadline" and made feeble attempts, a number of times, to change it into "lifeline." That didn't make much sense either, so I dropped it and continued about my daily business. Gideon, Marla and my dream faded into the background of my memory.

This evening it became dark earlier than usual. Black clouds, monster clouds, came from out of the east and covered the sky. Flashes of lightning and loud cracks of thunder split the air. I was reminded of mighty Thor hurling his angry thunderbolts at a cowering, frightened people. And then the rains came. The weather forecasters were saying that there would be heavy rain throughout the night. Radio and television stations were warning of flash floods and there was talk of tornados. It was unusual for us to have tornados in our area.

Malika, Jonathan and I sat watching the updated reports on television. I had never seen a tornado except in the movie *The Wizard of Oz*. I did not now, nor do I ever, want to see one in real life. What powerful forces they were, rampaging across the land, destroying everything in their paths. Our house sits somewhat higher off the road than the others in the neighborhood, and we are surrounded by tall pines and other large trees. I looked out the window and witnessed the trees swaying wildly in the wind. The storm had increased in its fury and would keep up this pace all night.

We all went to bed feeling anxious. Like all things, I thought, this, too, shall pass. I fell asleep listening to the howling of the wind and the sound of the rain as it beat against the windows. At about six o'clock the next morning, I awoke. It seemed as if the entire house were shaking. Somewhat frightened by the commotion, the children had rushed into my bedroom and were looking out through the window. It was already getting lighter as I got up and looked out on one of the most amazing scenes I have ever encountered.

The rain was a sheet of water and the wind blew with such force that a few tall trees in a neighbor's yard had already snapped in two. A tall, stately pine, not more than thirty feet from my window, swung to and fro like a pendulum gone berserk.

"Do you think it will fall on the house, if it breaks?" asked Malika, her voice bringing me back to the potential danger.

"It's possible," I said as calmly as I could.

"Aren't we supposed to go down to the basement, Daddy?" asked Jonathan. Just as he spoke, all the electricity went out.

"Yes, we are, Jonathan, but not just yet. I think everything will be fine." I spoke with the hope of reassuring them rather than with any real conviction. Another burst of thunder echoed around, and then I heard a voice in my head say, "A thousand shall fall at thy side, and ten thousand at thy right hand, but it shall not come nigh thee."

I repeated the words to myself, remembering that they came from the Book of Psalms. I made a mental note to check it out. The words persisted for a few more seconds, and then the entire house shook with another crack of thunder. I stood staring, an awestruck witness to the power of nature. A sudden calm came over me, and I knew with great certainty that all would be well.

The children, however, were becoming more frightened by the minute. I hugged them and said in a very soothing voice, "Come, now. There's no need to be afraid. This is quite an adventure. Enjoy it while it lasts." Somewhat reassured, they stood there for a while quietly calming their fears.

"We're not afraid, Daddy," said Jonathan. "We're just concerned about you." He smiled a confident smile and went back to play with his toy planes and space cruisers. In his innocent mind, he was riding above rain, wind and storms and was doing battle with the enemies of the galaxy. Malika simply said, "We'll make you breakfast today, Daddy."

"But there's no electricity," I said.

"It'll come back on shortly," she replied.

As they left the room and went to the kitchen, the electricity returned. I could hear the children shout and at the same time noticed that the trees were swaying less severely than before. Even the rain gradually became lighter, and within fifteen minutes all seemed back to normal. All, that is, except for the broken trees across the way. I quickly grabbed a jacket and went outside to survey what damage had been done. I expected to see the worst and stood there for a moment looking all around me. With the exception of a garbage can that had been blown into a neighbor's yard, there was no damage.

Yet, all around me were signs of destruction. Again the words "A thousand shall fall at thy side, and ten thousand at thy right hand, but it shall not come nigh thee" recurred to me. How comforting, I thought, and, also, how true. And then there were other voices. "Stand still and see the victory of Jehovah which He will work for you today." Finally, all was quiet. Those were biblical verses I had learned when I was in Sunday school. Nevertheless, there was great comfort in them. An overwhelming feeling of gratitude filled my heart, and all I could say was, "Thank you. Thank you for your help, once again."

Suddenly the sunlight broke through the clouds and flooded the area with warmth and hope. Birds appeared as if out of nowhere, and way off in the distance, the arc of a rainbow emerged, then slowly disappeared. I returned to the house and helped the children prepare breakfast.

A little later in the day, I drove around the neighborhood. Trees were down, power lines cut and debris scattered all over, but fortunately, no one was injured. Within a few days, most of these unfortunate situations would be corrected. There would be a lot of complaining, and some who had sustained more damage than others would look around and ask, "Why me?" Every time I hear someone say that, I cringe. "Why me, Lord? Why not the other guy? Why did you let me lose my job or my home or whatever?" How selfish we can be at times. Is it less terrible if it happens to someone else but more terrible if it happens to me?

The point, I surmised, is not that things happen to me or to others, but that things happen. It is for us to learn from what is happening and to know that it will not continue forever. Life is a flowing river—a river that's always changing. All things change and today's pauper could be tomorrow's prince, or today's indifference could be tomorrow's mourning. Even the weather is an indicator of the constancy of change. Last night and this morning, heavy rains and gale force winds; now, beautiful sunlight and gentle breezes. There will always be changes in the world, but something within me was saying that a part of me—a part of all of us—is changeless and beyond the reach of storms. That part has been with us from time immemorial, and in our quiet moments, if we listen carefully, we can hear it speaking to us.

That part of us which seems to know, which seems to be so silent and serene, that God-part placed there by our Creator is ever so loving, ever so kind and always our conscience and our guide. Somehow, I felt safe and sure of my world at this moment. I was not afraid of sequences of events or even consequences. I was just grateful that a whole new world was opening up to me as fast as it was.

Returning home, the first thing I heard was the phone ringing. These days, I am reluctant to answer it, much preferring to let the children do so. It is not that I dislike phones. There's a much simpler reason. Whenever I answer the phone, it usually is for one of the children, generally the child at the farthest corner of the house. There is a strange game the children play. Each one waits for the other to answer the call, and of course, it is never for the one who answers.

This time it was for me. Jonathan handed me the receiver.

"Hello," I said.

"Hi, John," said the voice on the other end. "I'm sorry to bother you at home, but a mutual friend gave me your number and said I should call you. My name is Karman, James Karman. Do you have a moment?"

"Why, sure," I responded. "I guess so."

"Could you help me? My friend said that you're always willing to help. You see, my son lost his job a few months ago. He's so depressed and it breaks my heart to see him suffering like this. He has a wife and two children. He's been looking for a new position but with no success. Is there anything you can suggest that would help?" The desperation in his voice was obvious. But why did he call me? I had no way of helping this man or his son. The pain and hopelessness in his voice reminded me of the time I stood by my own wife's bed, powerless to help her in her pain. Perhaps "hell" is watching a loved one suffer without being able to lift a finger to help.

"I'm so sorry about that," I said, "but I don't know if there is anything I can do about finding him a job. I wouldn't know where to begin. I've been away from the corporate life for years and have lost all my contacts there."

"No, no, John," he replied quickly. "I didn't mean for you to help him find a job. I meant to ask you if you would speak with him, help him find himself, give him a few pointers on how to keep going. From what our mutual friend said, you're very familiar with these situations. Please help him."

I felt a great compassion for this man and his son. Memories came to mind of how my dad wanted to help me when I was losing everything I owned. I remembered how he had been unable to give me even a little money to keep me going. But what he gave me was far greater than material wealth. He gave me courage and belief in myself. He helped me to see a far greater vision. How often in the past I had longed for someone to speak to, someone possessed with wisdom and compassion who could utter the one word or the one phrase to keep my hopes burning. And then there came Gideon, who taught me that we are all parts of the whole, all connected, and that we must always help one another, care for one another, love one another.

"James," I said, "I'll speak with your son. Ask him to call me as soon—"

"He's here with me," James said. "And if it's not too inconvenient, could you speak with him right now?"

"OK. Put him on. I'll see what I can do. By the way, James, who is this mutual friend who told you about me?"

"Well," James hesitated, "he really isn't a close friend. In fact, we only met once. I was sitting at a bar feeling really dejected. I must have been the picture of misery when this person walked in. He looked around, saw me, came up to me and asked if he could join me. We talked for a while and then he suggested that I call you. He said to tell you that his name was Gideon and that you would understand."

"Sure, sure," I said. "Gideon gets around. He's an old friend of mine." I made a mental note to ask Gideon what he meant by distributing my phone number to every stranger he met. By this time, the voice on the other end of the phone line had changed. I was now speaking with James Karman's son.

"Hello. My name is Jess Karman. My dad said that I should talk with you." He was more nervous than anyone I had spoken with in a long time. I immediately tried to set him at ease. Although I was a bit annoyed at having to deal with someone else's problem today, a voice kept reminding me that whenever I help others solve their problem, I am also solving my own.

"Jess, tell me what's going on with you. I understand that you're not working, that you lost your job." I attempted to be as understanding as possible.

Jess then launched into his story of how things were tough and corporations were not fair, of how he had worked so hard for so long, only to be replaced by someone who was less expensive for the company. He talked of his wife and children's suffering and even of how his poor dad had become involved. I listened sympathetically for a while. What he seemed to need most was someone to listen and care. We spoke for about an hour, and I pointed out to him the things for which he should be grateful—he had his family, his health, his youth, and if he could control his fear and regain his confidence, he would see success again.

"Listen, Jess," I said as I brought our conversation to an end. "Don't ever lose your sense of purpose. Just two things are necessary for success in this life. One is a sense of purpose and the other is a touch of madness. These are the two most important ingredients in the recipe for success. Face your fears and deal with them. All fear is precipitated by a consideration of loss. You've only lost a job. But the right job is waiting for you. Believe in your God and believe in yourself. Things are working out for you. Keep me posted."

As I hung up the phone, I had a feeling of satisfaction at being able to help someone. I enjoyed a sense of satisfaction that I was able to spend a little time helping a fellow traveler along the road of life. Now the ancient truths came clearly to my mind once again. It is by helping others that we are helped, it is by giving that we receive, and it is by loving that we are loved.

CHAPTER
13

Why Walk on Water
When You Can Fly?

Long ago, I roamed the hamlets of foreign countries, tasting the joys of various cultures and basking in the broadening experience of international travel. It is a strange life that I have led. It has taken me across oceans and continents, through jungles and plains and into the presence of princes and fishermen, rich and poor. I have been to many places, have seen and experienced many things, but one place I have never visited is the place where someone else stands—not physically, I mean, but in a more emotional and spiritual sense.

Most of our wars, most of our conflicts, whether in a grand, worldwide scale or in a simpler, more ordinary, everyday manner, are primarily due to our tendency to judge others. How easy it has been for me, for example, to sit back in self-righteous indignation and cling tenaciously to my point of view to the detriment of all else.

People do things for reasons that are so personal and individual that even they, themselves, do not understand why. I am reminded of the seeker of truth who took off all his clothes at lunchtime and jumped into an icy pond. As soon as he emerged, which was almost instantaneously, an observer asked him why he had done such a stupid thing. His answer, I believe, contained great wisdom, as he declared, "It seemed like a good idea at the time."

Whatever we have done, we did because it seemed like a good idea at the time. The trick is to learn from past mistakes and to correct our present and future actions, to evolve into a higher order of being and to let compassion, love, joy and understanding flourish. As this occurs, we begin to become more tolerant of all those around us. A new power arises within, and we find that circumstances and events are powerless to harm us. Upon this awareness, a new and brighter day dawns.

Ever since my first meeting with Gideon, I have tried to live a life exemplifying many of the principles he taught me. There were times when I succeeded brilliantly, times when everything seemed to work so well that I wondered how I could ever not have known what to do in crisis situations. But there were times, many of them, when, no matter what I did, nothing went right. I would then fret and fume, thinking all the while that there was no sense or purpose to human existence. As I persisted in practicing, changes would occur, and again, the matter that had seemed so impossible would work itself out in ways that were too perfect to explain. I also became aware that whenever I switched focus from my problems to those of others, whenever I tried to help others instead of being immersed in my own misery, events took a decided turn for the better.

This day, as I sat on my porch, a gentle breeze arose and a penetrating silence descended. The temperature dropped a few degrees, but I remained there, ever so tranquil, ever so peaceful, watching the interplay of nature. Tomorrow I would be taking a trip to the Big City for routine business purposes. Visiting the Big City was always an exciting experience for me, and it had been a long time since my last trip. I was really looking forward to the experience. It would not be a long trip, only a day—leaving in the morning and returning later in the evening—with a flight time of about two hours.

Sitting there enjoying the breeze, the serenity and thoughts of the Big City, I felt at one with my world. This, indeed, was relaxation. This was the "bliss at eventide." The tensions and stresses of the day dropped away from me, like magnets that seemed to have lost their strength. I drank in the cool evening air and sat there, not concentrating on anything special, but allowing my mind and body to be as one. Within a few minutes I felt so refreshed that I decided to go inside and pack for my trip.

I spent some time with the children and then started preparing for the next day. There was little to do, and since tomorrow would be a long day, we turned in early. Sleep is a gift. It calms the troubled heart and restores to the human mind and body the necessary strength and energy to continue living one day at a time. I must have slept well, for when I woke up I was totally refreshed and ready to go.

I arrived at the airport on schedule, checked in and boarded my plane. This was an early flight, and I was pleasantly surprised to find that I had an empty seat next to me. I always enjoy adjacent seats that are vacant, although I'm sure the airlines look at it differently. There were not only empty seats on both sides of me but in front of me and behind me as well. How comfortable, I thought, not being crushed like sardines.

After we took off, I adjusted the seat and prepared to enjoy the flight. I have always loved to fly. Ever since I can remember, I have been reading stories about flying. At the age of sixteen, I almost ran away from home to join the Royal Air Force in England. It was only my father's wisdom and my mother's compassionate pleas that persuaded me not to go. Since then, I have mastered a few flying lessons but find myself more comfortable flying in commercial jumbo jets rather than small, single-engine planes.

A light tap on my shoulder caught my attention and I turned around, only to behold the friendly faces of Gideon and Marla. It was Gideon who spoke first.

"We thought you wouldn't mind if we sat with you for a while, John."

"Going to the Big City also?" I asked.

Ignoring my question, Gideon said, "I am glad you have some empty seats next to you. Do you mind if we sit?"

"Sure, sure, sit," I said.

"We are both on our way to the Big City," said Marla as both she and Gideon took the seats next to me, one on my right and the other on my left, like armed guards holding a captive prisoner.

"I didn't know you were going to be on this flight," I said. "I didn't see you at the airport even though I was there early and certainly would not have missed you. Did you arrive late?"

"We are never late," responded Gideon. "We arrived here on time, didn't we?"

"Here? On the plane?" I asked.

"Of course, John," he said. "We heard that you were going to be on this flight, and since we had a meeting at Headquarters, we figured we'd join you and keep you company for a while. Always good to see a friend."

"But how did you get on the plane?" I asked.

"Listen," said Marla, "why walk on water when you can fly?"

"John," said Gideon, "there are ways of traveling with which you are not yet acquainted. We are here and that's what's important. How long are you staying in the Big City?"

"I'm coming back this evening. How long will you be there?"

"We'll return this evening or tomorrow. It doesn't matter. We're having a regional meeting at Headquarters. Should only last a few hours. You remember our Headquarters, don't you? You visited a few years ago."

"Of course, I remember. Meeting God and all that. Is He still around?"

"Where else would He be?" replied Marla.

"Sometimes I wonder," I muttered to myself.

"Always cynical, aren't you, John?" Gideon observed. He continued without waiting for my response. "Will you have any free time? Perhaps we could meet for a little while. You need some relaxation."

"I'll be free after my meeting," I said.

"Why don't you come to Headquarters with us this afternoon?" Marla asked. "Our meeting won't be long, and we'll be able to spend some time together before you return to the airport. That should work out just fine. What do you say, John? The chief will be there, too."

"The last time I was there, it was glorious and frightening all at the same time, but I'd love to go. It's not every day one meets with God, you know."

"Not every day, but every hour and every second, you meet God. Sometimes He worries about you. He has asked us a number of times to bring you again for a short visit. He thinks you need the inspiration and a closer look at the company." Marla looked at me and nodded as if that explained everything.

"God worries about me?" I asked, somewhat puzzled. "I didn't think God worried. Only people worry. And He has asked about me? He certainly has a lot of better things to do than to concern Himself with me. There are over five billion of us on earth you know."

Gideon took up the conversation. "By saying that God worries about you, we do not mean that He is a worrier. Marla meant that God is concerned about your progress on earth. He wants you to fulfill your mission, to accomplish the purpose for which you came to earth. He is concerned because He loves and cares about you. He wants you to succeed."

"It is difficult to understand how such a powerful, almighty One could have time for trivial human pursuits. Sometimes, in my less enlightened moments I fail to understand how God could love us, care for us and help us."

"You don't always have to understand, John," replied Gideon. "It is more important that you accept it. Remember the scriptures? God cares about sparrows, about lilies of the field, about everything."

"Seems to me," I said, "that we've had this conversation before. It always ends the same way. I've got a few things I would like to ask God this time."

"Why don't you ask Him this afternoon? You'll be seeing Him. But then again, you don't always like His answers," said Gideon.

"By the way," I asked, "do you really think I'll have enough time to visit your Headquarters and still catch my plane?"

Marla and Gideon simultaneously broke into laughter. I looked at them with a puzzled expression. Having regained their composure, they looked at each other, and Gideon said, "It's really funny, Marla. Here is this man who'll be meeting with God this afternoon. He'll be speaking directly with the Almighty, the Lord of Creation, and he's worried about whether or not he'll miss his plane."

Marla turned to me and said, "I'm sorry, John. Both Gideon and I got carried away by the ludicrous nature of the situation. It's just that the entire earth scene seems pretty absurd at times. People scurrying to their synagogues, temples or churches for an hour or so and then rushing back home, not having time for anything. Patiently God stands by, always watching and waiting, ever trying to help. But how could He help when no one is listening? He doesn't interfere in our freedom of choice, you see. We must be willing and trusting. We must listen for that 'still, small voice,' which speaks to us from the deepest parts of our soul."

Gideon added, "You'll have another opportunity today to ask God whatever you'd like to ask. As for catching your plane? Don't worry, no problem. We guarantee that you'll be home with your children tonight."

"Sometimes I wonder about the two of you," I said, more as a loving comment than as a critical remark.

"We'll see you after your meeting," said Gideon.

"Here, let me give you the address," I said, reaching into my pocket for a pen and a piece of paper.

"We know where you'll be, John. We'll find you," he said.

Our conversation continued until the captain announced that we would soon be landing. From this altitude the Big City appeared so peaceful that one could almost believe it to be sleeping. Yet, it was a hive of activity at all hours of the day and night. In a few minutes we would be on the ground.

Gideon stood up and said, "We must get back to our assigned seats, John. We'll see you later."

Marla followed him, smiling as she passed by. "See you soon," she said as they both proceeded to the rear of the plane.

It was a textbook landing, with hardly a ripple as we touched down and taxied to the gate. A few minutes later, we prepared to disembark. There was no need for rushing, since we had arrived right on schedule. I thought I'd remain in my seat for a short while to wait for Marla and Gideon. By this time the plane was almost empty, but I was sure that they could not have passed by without my seeing them. A few minutes later I stood up and looked around. I was the only one left on the plane.

Marla and Gideon had done it again. They had completely disappeared into thin air. Not at all surprised, I picked up my small travel bag, adjusted my tie and exited the plane. An hour and a half later, I arrived at the hotel where my meeting was to be held. It would last about an hour. After that I would be meeting with the president and chairman of the board of G&M Enterprises, Inc.!

CHAPTER
14

The Shadow of the Almighty

All went well, and after dealing with some general questions about routine business matters, the meeting came to an end. I said good-bye and then quickly made my way through the lobby and out of the hotel. There, leaning against a lamppost, stood Gideon. Marla was waiting next to him. I approached them.

"Marla, Gideon!" I shouted above the noise of the city.

"Hi, John," said Marla. "Right on time."

"Good," said Gideon. "Let's go to our next appointment."

"You found me again," I said.

"Sometimes it's easier to find others than to find

ourselves," Gideon replied with that old penetrating smile.

I followed them to a waiting taxi, and within a few minutes we found ourselves in front of an impressive building located on a side street. Gideon paid the fare, and we got out and walked through the door into the lobby. We took the first available elevator to the thirty-third floor. I remembered this from years earlier and was somewhat surprised that nothing had changed. We walked into the reception room, where Marla asked us to sit. She went to the receptionist, whispered something in hushed tones and rejoined us.

"We'll soon be in the presence of the Chief," she said.

Only now did the full impact of what we were doing strike me. Once again, I would be meeting with God face to face. Once again, I would have the opportunity to ask Him questions concerning the past, present and future. Perhaps He would explain to me why we go through life struggling at every turn. Perhaps He would even tell me about Mardai and why she had to leave this life at such a young age. My thoughts were running wild when Gideon's voice brought me back to the present moment.

"John," he said in a kind and loving way, "you're a bit nervous. Calm yourself. This meeting will do you quite some good. There's nothing to be afraid of. If anything, you'll leave here feeling more confident and more in control of the events in your life."

"Yes," Marla joined in. "Ask God any questions you want. He never refuses to answer, although, sometimes,

He does not offer explanations. This can be frustrating, but you'll learn a lot."

"I've longed to see Him again," I said. "There are so many things I want to know and, yet, all the questions I had are gone from my mind. This is ridiculous, you know."

Before either one could answer, the receptionist came over and spoke. "You may go in now. The usual meeting room, Gideon."

"Thanks, Mary," said Gideon as he stood up. Marla and I followed him down a well-lit hallway to a door marked "President and Chairman of the Board." Gideon knocked, turned the door knob and entered. I followed behind Marla. The office was elegant and unpretentiously decorated, and if I remembered correctly, it had the same celestial blue carpeting. The large desk and the office files, however, were gone. It seemed more like a living room than an office.

As we stood there, the door at the opposite end opened and in walked a beautiful young woman. I have seen many gorgeous women in my lifetime, but never had I seen one as ravishing as this creature approaching us. She must be God's secretary or assistant, I surmised. She seemed to flow into the room with a grace usually possessed by royalty. Her long dress radiated with the colors of the rainbow and her hair accentuated the beauty of her face. This must be the most exquisite woman in the universe. Finding myself spellbound by her beauty, I just stared at her.

"Please sit," she said with a gentle voice and a warm smile. We all made ourselves comfortable, Gideon and Marla on the sofa while I took the straight-back chair. The woman sat on the floor in front of us. This seemed odd, since there were other vacant chairs about. No one had bothered to introduce us, but I assumed that was an oversight. I noticed Marla and Gideon looking at me with what could possibly be called amusement. I, personally, didn't see anything funny in the situation.

"Well, John," said Gideon. "What are you thinking?"

"Thinking? I'm not really thinking about anything. Why don't you introduce me to this beautiful lady?" I asked.

"Oh, I'm sorry," replied Marla. "I thought you knew her. You've met many times before and she knows you. John, please meet God."

"God?" I stammered, looking at the lady sitting so quietly on the floor in front of me. "God? You aren't God, are you?"

Her voice was music itself as she answered. "It must have puzzled you that I'm in the form of a female today. You're so used to thinking of me as male. I just returned from visiting a culture where I am thought of as *Mother God* instead of *Father God*. There are a number of such cultures, you know. But if it would make you feel more comfortable, you could see me as male. It really doesn't matter to me. I am male, female, neither, both, whatever. I am *everything*. There cannot be two *everything*."

By this time Marla and Gideon were laughing. Gideon

managed to compose himself first. "Please forgive us, John," he said. "We felt that this setting would prove to be of interest to you. It was God who suggested it. Sometimes it's fun bringing excitement and humor into life."

I was appalled at their seeming lack of respect in the presence of God. In many of God's churches, laughter was not looked upon with favor. Centuries ago, you would have been burned at the stake for such behavior. The voice of God interrupted my thoughts.

"John," said She, "most people misunderstand me. This is a happy universe. I created it so. I wanted all my creation to be joyous. Although I am God, sometimes even I can't understand why people are so scared of me. Of course, some of your churches have been teaching their followers that I am a vengeful, angry being, that I am ready to punish anyone for even the smallest infraction of rules I don't even recall making. It's silly, of course. Come now, we have a lot to talk about."

God stopped speaking and stood up. I was watching very closely because it's not every day that one has such an experience as this. As I stared at Her, Her body became blurred and I squinted my eyes in an effort to focus. Then, a split second later, She changed into the form of a male. I held my breath for a few seconds and reasoned to myself that I'd be waking up shortly and all this would have been just a bizarre dream, not real at all.

"This is real, John," God said. "But it's also a dream, although not in the way you normally think. Also, since this culture thinks of me as male, I have assumed the form of a male. And sure, I know your thoughts. I know everybody's thoughts when I want to know them. You were also thinking that it's not every day that one has an audience with me. Well, you're wrong there. Every day, every hour, every second one can have access to me. I am in every part of my creation and every part of it is in me. And about this male-female situation, it really isn't important. There are many more important matters to deal with than trying to figure out whether I am male or female, black or white, yellow or red, Christian or Jew, Hindu or Muslim. I am all of these and more."

"Then what about the Father, Son and Holy Spirit?" I asked.

"In some cultures that is what is preferred. In others it is Mother, Daughter and Holy Spirit. In still others it is Creator, Preserver and Destroyer. How about Creator, Child and the Whole of Spirit? It doesn't matter. God is *One*. But each life-form perceives me differently. Come, let's go visit one of my favorite spots."

Suddenly, the room disappeared and we found ourselves at the top of a very high mountain. I looked around and saw the ocean in the distance. The waters were a gentle shade of bluish green. "Yes, John," said God, "you may call this a mountaintop experience. You don't have to come up to the mountain to see me. You climb mountains to find *you*. Stay close to me and your difficulties cease to be of mountainous proportions."

I knew He was trying to teach me something very

important, but I was not quite sure what it was. It didn't matter, however, because I so enjoyed being with Him or Her. There is a peace beyond description whenever one is with God. There's a bliss that surpasses all imagination when you're in the presence of the Almighty. Perhaps, this was what the Psalmist meant when he said, "He who dwells in the secret place of the Most High shall abide under the Shadow of the Almighty."

We stood there for a long while enjoying the wind, the sun, the panoramic view. No one uttered a sound. A cloud or two passed by, and high atop this mountain could be heard the songs of little birds as they flitted among the branches of evergreen trees. God stood next to me and I glanced at Him from the corner of my eye. His hair appeared blond, but a closer look revealed it to be somewhat darker. He wore a sweatshirt and blue jeans that were faded in spots. I looked again at His hair and this time it appeared gray. It was the strangest thing, His hair changing color like that.

"If it bothers you, John, I'll let it remain one color," God offered solicitously.

"It's not the hair," I said. "I was just thinking how peaceful it is to be with you, how the experience of being in your Presence is so blissful."

"You *should* have this experience every day," He replied. "You could set the tone for your entire day by recalling experiences such as this when you awake in the morning. Some people call it prayer, others think of it as meditation or contemplation. I am always as close to you as your thoughts. Think of me and you are instantly in touch. That's how close I am to you. And, remember, you never see me as *I am*, you always see me as *you are*."

"You mean that You are not as You appear to be right now?" I was a bit puzzled.

"This is only one of the many possible ways I appear. What I mean is that most of humanity thinks of me in certain ways and believes that I am what they think. Take some of the ancient civilizations, for example. They believed that I was a jealous, angry, vengeful God existing only to be worshipped and feared. And as they believed, so it was."

"What You are saying, Lord, goes against many of the things we've been taught," I said.

"Do you always believe everything that you've been taught, John?" He asked.

Marla and Gideon were quietly listening to us. God raised His left hand and pointed in a wide circle. "Look," He said. "Look at all this beauty. The earth is very special to me. All my worlds are special, but I have a soft spot in my heart for earth. You ought to enjoy more of its beauty. Spend more time with its rivers, lakes, mountains and forests. It's easier for us to converse in places like this. Care for your environment. Don't think that if you pollute it, it would be destroyed. No, it would destroy you, instead."

As soon as He stopped speaking, the entire scenery around us shimmered and disappeared. In a split second we were back at the offices of G&M Enterprises, Inc. It seemed as if we had never left. We were even sitting in the same positions as before. It certainly was exciting being with God—strange, but exciting.

"Lord," I said, "I have been waiting these many years to ask You questions of great importance to me. Yet, when I'm in Your Presence, the questions don't seem important. Everything seems to be just fine when I am near You."

"Why don't you practice being in my presence more often? Why can't you be near me whenever you so desire? I am always close to you," He said.

"I haven't gone to church in quite a while, Lord. I usually miss a few Sundays each month. I guess I'll go more often now."

"I, myself, haven't gone recently," He said. "I think I'll have to visit some of them to see what they're up to."

I almost fell out of my chair. I thought that perhaps I hadn't heard Him correctly. But I remained quiet as He continued. "It's not that I don't like some aspects of church. The music is usually good and I do enjoy the singing. But think of it, John, century after century of listening to the same thing. Preachers shouting doom and gloom from their pulpits. Congregations being frightened into believing ridiculous arguments about me and my intentions. Each group, sect or denomination claiming to know the right way. Imagine listening to what is called 'The Lord's Prayer' hundreds of millions of times a week. Only once in a while do I hear someone say it with feelings. All the rest is just noise and meaningless babble. The same goes for the whole worship situation.

"The point I want to make is that although rituals have their place, what is more important is what we do for one another, how much we love and help one another. I do not care for incense or worship as much as I care for people, animals, trees and the other aspects of my creation. When the intent is to give service to the inhabitants of your world, then you'll truly find your peace. Then will you come to truly know yourself and, in so doing, know me better." His voice trailed into a whisper as He turned to Gideon and Marla and said, "It's time to get John back to his home."

"But, Lord," I argued, "I still have so many questions. Can't we . . . ?"

"I know. You want to ask about Mardai, about your dad, your children, your work and all your other concerns. I will meet with you again in a short while and we'll go over some of those questions. But for now, you need to return to your regular schedule. You have a plane to catch and your children are waiting to see you. Marla and Gideon will see you back to the airport."

God walked over and threw His arm around my shoulder as He led me to the door. Gideon and Marla followed behind us. "Don't forget now, John," God said, "to just practice being in the presence of God. Find that secret place where the troubles of your world cannot touch you. And, yes," He added as an afterthought, "He who dwells in the secret place of the Most High shall abide under the Shadow of the Almighty. I'll have a special treat for you soon. *Vaya con Dios.*" A few seconds later, He was gone.

Marla decided to remain at G&M Enterprises for a while but promised that she would call me soon. Gideon and I took the elevator down to the first floor, caught a cab and went directly to the airport. We didn't speak much. I believe that he wanted me to assimilate most of what had happened today. He said good-bye and promised to be in touch. A few hours later, I had left the Big City far behind me. There was a sweet sadness in leaving my dear friends, but I knew that today I had experienced a most "learningful" adventure, and I couldn't wait for our next meeting.

CHAPTER
15

Color My Attic Green

The following week was spent catching up with all the little tasks I had left undone. The memory of my visit with God was fresh in my mind, and I made even greater efforts to practice being in His presence. I regretted not being able to obtain any specific information about Mardai, but I was content with the thought that I would soon find out more.

Saturday arrived, and I found myself experiencing a strong undercurrent of excitement. Upon closer examination, I could not find any reason for being so happy, and yet, it was a feeling I couldn't shake. Sometimes I become miserable when I'm apparently happy for no reason, because I "rationally" figure that there is nothing to be happy about. It was only recently that I realized that you don't need a reason to be happy. In the middle of my reflections, the phone rang. I picked it up and said, "Hello."

"Hi, John, this is Gideon."

"Hi, Gideon. I've missed you and Marla," I said.

As usual, he got straight to the point. "Today, you'll have a visit from the Almighty. Remember our last meeting when He promised you a treat? Well, this is the day."

"Hold on, hold on, Gideon!" I fairly shouted. "Start over again from the beginning. What's all this about?"

Gideon paused for a moment and then said, "God's coming to your house today. Marla and I will be with Him, of course."

"God's coming to see me? Why would He do that?"

"You went to see Him, didn't you? Why shouldn't He come to see you? After all, you *are* trying to get closer to Him."

"Yes, I know, but this all sounds so strange. God coming to my house? I can't believe it."

"You probably are wondering what the neighbors will think. Well, don't let that bother you. He visits their homes, too, but most of them never see Him or acknowledge His presence. What with all that concern about yard work, the cleaning, cooking, laundry and, of course, the children, who has time for God?"

"I see you're trying to be funny, Gideon," I said. "I'll

always have time for God. It's an honor to have Him visit. By the way, what do you mean that God visits the neighbors' homes, too?"

"He visits all homes, but not all see Him. He speaks to all, but not all hear. He has visited your home so many times that it is almost as if He lives there. He also lives in your neighbors' homes, in homes in every town and village. He lives everywhere, John."

"If He lives here, why, then, does He have to visit? Stop talking in riddles, Gideon, and please answer in simple sentences," I said.

"I wasn't jesting," he replied in a more serious tone of voice. "I was just trying to get you to think. The simplicity of the matter is that God is everywhere, but not everyone is aware of His presence. Later today, He will visit you in a way that will always remind you of His closeness. It seems that you always have to see to believe, but I tell you, believe and you will see."

"Then I'd better get busy and mow the lawn and straighten the—"

He did not let me finish. "No, no. There's no need for special preparations. You don't have to do anything out of the ordinary. God always sees you as you are and as you can be."

"At least," I said, "I should pick up some cake and some fresh ground coffee."

Gideon's laugh resounded through the telephone. "I am sure that coffee and cakes are high on God's priority list of concerns," he said. "Come on, John, forget about those things, just expect God's visit this afternoon, around, shall we say, four o'clock. Will that timing suit you?"

"Anytime God wants to visit me suits me just fine," I responded nervously. "But, Gideon, what about the children? Will they be able to meet Him, too?"

"Children meet God more often than adults do. Yours see Him every day. But today, they won't be able to see Him. His main business is with you. Marla and I have made some other arrangements for Malika and Jonathan. They'll both be spending the night at their friends' home."

"I'll have to tell them about this."

"The arrangements have already been made, so don't worry, just go about your work as if nothing's happening," he said.

"As if nothing's happening? God's coming to my house and you tell me to do my work as if nothing's happening?"

He interrupted again. "You seem to miss the point, John. God has always been at your house, so why make such a big fuss? The only difference is that this time, you'll be aware of His presence. Your house or the Headquarters of G&M Enterprises, what difference does it make?"

"I'll be ready, Gideon," I said.

"See you later, my friend," he replied and hung up the phone.

Before I could collect my thoughts, the children came in. They had been playing outdoors for the past hour, and since it was close to lunchtime, I assumed they were hungry.

"You ask him, Malika," said Jonathan with an impish grin.

"Daddy," said Malika, "would you let Jonathan and me stay over at Lisa's place tonight? Lisa's brother, Mark, will watch a movie with Jonathan. They'll be real good, Daddy. Lisa and I will keep an eye on them. Please, Daddy, can we spend the night, please?"

They both seemed so excited. "When did this come up?" I asked. "You didn't ask me about it before."

"Mark and Lisa just asked us a few minutes ago. They said that it was okay with their parents," answered Jonathan.

Naturally, I granted them permission and immediately called Mark and Lisa's parents to confirm these arrangements. Around three o'clock, Malika and Jonathan packed their little overnight bags and went next door to spend the evening with their friends. I was left alone, wondering exactly what to do when God arrived.

I shuffled around the house for a while, not knowing quite what to expect. I went outside thinking that I would ask practical questions of God instead of all the silly, mundane questions I tended to propose when I was with Him. This would be my opportunity. This time I would not be put off by answers that seemed too vague or complex. Perhaps He'd walk around the yard with me and give me some tips on how to get the mimosa tree to spread its branches. I know, I grinned, I'll ask Him about the leaking pipe in the basement and at the same time check His opinion on whether I should resurface the driveway or not.

The more I thought about it, the more I realized how many things I would like God to help me with. Of course, there are those two bad tires on the car. I wonder if I should replace them now or keep them for another few months or so. Then there is the matter of sending the children to spend some vacation time with their grandparents. Should this be done early in the summer or much later, preferably a few weeks before the new school year begins? I must not forget the room in the attic. Surely God would agree that I should paint it. But what color should I use? Perhaps green . . . or maybe yellow or blue. No problem—God will help me with all these decisions.

And so it went, each question becoming more meaningless and self-centered than the one before. It took me just a few minutes to realize that I had fallen into an old but senseless habit. With an embarrassed smile, I discovered that I didn't need to ask God about my mimosa tree. The information was readily available at the nursery or library, and a phone call or visit would teach me all I needed to know. Our local plumber could advise me concerning the basement pipe, and it didn't require much common sense to figure that the tires should be checked by the mechanic at the gas station I usually patronize. As for the children spending a week with their grandpar-

ents, why didn't I just call and ask the grandparents
which week would be best?

It is interesting how we can solve many of our
problems by just realizing that we already possess most
of the information we need. Imagine asking God about
the color of paint I should use in the attic! The next thing
I wanted to check would probably have been whether
God preferred me to get a haircut this week or next. As
I mulled these things over in my mind, it became clear to
me that any color I chose for the room in the attic would
be fine. If I preferred blue, then blue was excellent. If
green made me happy, than I should color my attic
green. It was up to me to decide what to do about
haircuts, tires and such matters.

I slowly walked back to the house, thinking how we
look to God to solve so many problems we ourselves are
well equipped to handle. It seemed to me that it was
better simply to do all we could about the problem and
then leave the rest to God. The Creator has already
provided us with the tools we need for living. All we
have to do is make an effort to find and use them
properly.

It was approaching four o'clock and God would be
arriving soon. I had started out trying to figure what
questions to ask Him. How could I have forgotten to
think of asking for some help for old Mrs. Jones, whose
husband had recently died? And yes, I should have
considered offering assistance to that family who lost
everything in a house fire the other day. I definitely

should solicit God's aid for those in greater need than
myself. Next to their problems mine seemed so insignif-
icant. However, this time, I will also ask about Mardai
and her life.

With these thoughts, I pulled out the coffee pot,
started a fresh brew and sat down at the kitchen table to
await the coming of God.

CHAPTER
16

I Can See Clearly Now

I hadn't been sitting for more than a few moments when the doorbell rang. I jumped out of my chair, rushed to the front door and excitedly jerked it open. I was so anxious to see God again, but He wasn't there. It was Gideon, cheerful as usual. Even Marla was not there.

"Come in, Gideon," I said. "It's good to see you, but where is God and where is Marla?"

"Marla came up the back stairs to the porch. She said that it was such a beautiful day, you probably wouldn't mind if we all sit out on the porch and enjoy the gifts of nature as we talk."

"That's fine with me," I replied. "But where is God? It's already four o'clock."

"God is never late," said Gideon, and the moment he spoke, the phone rang.

"Go ahead, Gideon, pour yourself a cup of coffee. Pour me one, too, please. I'll be through with the phone in a few seconds."

Picking up the receiver, I said "Hello" and listened as a neighbor asked if I could lend him my electric drill. At first, I felt an obvious annoyance at his call, because I didn't want anything to keep me from my appointment with God. Then I realized that it's also important to do whatever one can to help others. There are so many of us who, when we hear of someone needing help, are prone to form a discussion committee rather than actively doing something about it.

"Sure," I said. "It's in the garage on the long bench; help yourself. Take it whenever you want. The door is open. Please excuse me. I have company and I've got to go now. Good-bye."

I turned back to Gideon, who said, "Let's go and sit with Marla on the porch."

"OK. I'll take her a cup of coffee," I replied.

"She prefers water, John. I'll get her a glass."

A few moments later, we were sitting with Marla on the porch. I was expecting God's arrival any moment now.

"Hello, John," Marla greeted me. "This is a wonderful setting for a meeting with Him."

"It certainly is," I responded, "but where is He, Marla? This is supposed to be the day, isn't it?"

"Yes, it's today and the time is right." Then, turning to Gideon, she said, "Why don't you go ahead and explain, Gideon."

"Relax, John," said Gideon. "I have a few things to tell you."

"I knew it! I knew it!" I shouted, disappointment welling up within me. "Something told me that He wouldn't be here." I breathed a sigh of resignation. Marla and Gideon said nothing for a short while. Finally, Gideon took another sip of coffee, leaned back in his chair and started speaking.

"Listen carefully, John," he said. "God didn't disappoint you. God never disappoints anyone. Remember, I told you earlier that God is never late? He did come. He's here, but He chose to do it in a different manner from the way you saw Him recently. He wanted you to realize that You didn't have to go to the Big City to see Him, that He's always with you and that an appointment is not necessary. He *is* here and with you this very moment, but you can't see as well as you can feel."

"Then, where is He, Gideon?" My voice was still laden with disappointment.

It was Marla who spoke next. "Listen, John, will you trust us for a little while longer?"

"Of course, Marla. You know that I've always trusted you and Gideon—or at least, almost always."

"Well, then," she said while pointing toward the trees,

"look around you, look all around you and become really quiet. Still those thoughts of yours that are running wild. Now listen to what your heart is saying and you'll begin to see God."

She seemed to be so concerned, so caring, and her voice was so soothing, that I sat silently for a time looking at the woods. Slowly at first and then with total absorption, my entire body started to relax. An overwhelming feeling of peace came over me and I smiled at Gideon. I even winked at Marla.

"It's fine," I whispered. "I know where He is."

"I think we've finally gotten through to him, Gideon," Marla announced proudly.

"I think so," was Gideon's reply.

"Yes, my dear friends," I said, "God is right here with me. He is in my heart, my very mind and soul. I don't have to go anywhere to find Him. All I have to do is to be quiet and I can hear Him speak to me. Now I know what you meant when you said that God is always here, that He visits my home, that He never leaves me. At first, I knew with my head, but now I know with my heart. Please, forgive me for not seeing this earlier. I just wonder why it took so long."

"Nothing to forgive, John," said Gideon. "Each of us eventually finds our God. For some, it happens quickly, but for others it may take a long, long time. You have really done well, John."

Gideon reached into the inside pocket of his jacket and pulled out an envelope. Handing it to me, he said, "This letter is for you, John. God wanted me to deliver it to you personally."

I took the letter and mumbled a grateful "Thank you." Written on a blue envelope were the words "To John with love—Open immediately." It was signed "G." I carefully opened the envelope and pulled out the contents. I glanced at Gideon, who said, "Read it now, John. Read it aloud, if you wish. We were present when He wrote it."

I leaned back in my chair, making myself a bit more comfortable, and started reading.

"Dear, Beloved John . . . You were expecting me to visit you in the same physical form as when you saw me last. This time, I chose not to do it that way but to show you that I am with you always and in many different forms and ways. At first, you were disappointed when I didn't arrive with Gideon and Marla. Actually, I was here before they arrived. I was always here, even before the Earth, the Universe or anything.

"Someone once told you that I am not like human beings, that I do not have arms, legs, a face and other human characteristics. To a certain extent, that is true because I am like anything that I want to be. I am the sum total of everything. I am *All That Is*. If I choose to be an invisible force or a field of interaction, then, that is what *I Am*. When I choose to be in human form, *I Am* that also. Sometimes it is difficult for you to conceive of me as just a benign force. When those times occur, it is better for you to see me or think of me in human terms.

It will help you to be closer to me. It will give you more comfort and strength, and as you grow in wisdom and understanding, you'll find that you no longer need to see or relate to me in any particular form, shape or size. You will then discover that you and I have always been together and that we are inseparable parts of each other.

"I was intrigued and pleased at your reflections on life as you roamed around your yard this afternoon. You don't need me to tell you what color to paint a room or what suit to wear to a meeting. Those are decisions most of my children can make without much difficulty. All you need to do is to practice being aware of me at all times. Yes, I have many children. There are many of you on earth, all uniquely different from one another. There are others who live in distant galaxies and in alternate spacetime universes. Each one is dear to me.

"Throughout your earth history there have been certain groups who claimed me for their own. They called other groups 'heathens' or 'unbelievers' and even started horrible wars to protect me from those who did not believe in me. Remember the crusades with King Richard against Saladin and his muslim followers? Both sides were fighting for me; both leaders wanted to save The Holy City for me. Consider how silly that was. I am God and don't need anyone to save me or protect me. I can do an excellent job by myself.

"Even in this, your twentieth century, there are so many religions, so many denominations, so many differences, each one thinking that it has found the only true

God. I have told you before that there is only one God and *I Am He* or *She* or *It*. Yes, I have many children on earth with names like Catholic, Protestant, Fundamentalist, Jew, Hindu, Muslim, Buddhist, Agnostic, Atheist and on and on. I love them all. Even though some of them do not believe in me, I believe in them and care for them equally. Should a father or mother love one child and hate the other? The parent wants the child to realize its full potential and to be happy and successful. That's what I want for all my children.

"At this point in my letter, you are probably wishing and hoping that I would say something about your beloved Mardai. There are many things you do not yet understand. Does a professor teach advanced algebra to a student in third grade? No. As you grow and learn, you will be able to understand the beauty of the Eternal Plan. But I will tell you this. Mardai is happy in her new work. She is as radiantly beautiful and gracious as when she was with you in physical form. Because of the different worlds you both occupy, you cannot see or hear her as you used to. There is a common meeting place, however, and just as you found me in your heart, there will you find her, also. She is pleased with your progress and she stays close to you. You will see her again when your work on earth is done. Know this, that the bonds that bind the two of you span eternity itself.

"Speak to her in your quiet moments, even as you speak to me. She will hear and answer. Don't worry so much about the children. They receive much help from us. Teach them the things you have learned and they'll be well equipped to fulfill their missions in life.

"Love one another. Forgive those who have harmed you or tried to take advantage of you. Let go of whatever resentments you may harbor for others. Forgive others, not because they deserve it, but because you do. Help one another, comfort and bless one another and, above all else, spend some time every day trying to be aware of my presence with you. As you practice, you will find that you draw yourself nearer to me. As you draw nearer, you will notice that you become happier and more successful in your work here on earth.

"I am not saying that you will never have any problems or that you'll never experience pain or seeming failure. All I'm saying is that even when the road seems rough, you will overcome. There will be tough times but not nearly as many as there have been. There will be failures, but failures are only failures because you don't see the larger picture; they are actually stepping stones to success. Tough times could also be glorious times.

"You must now continue with your work. Deep within you is a knowing of why you're here. When you are puzzled or frustrated, find a quiet spot where you can sit and talk with me. I have always been, and will always be, with you. I never abandon my children. Let my strength be your strength and my joy be your joy. You can see clearly now. The fog is lifting.

"Gideon and Marla will be around whenever you need them. They will not perform your miracles for you, but they will help you and show you how to do them yourself. They are your helpers here on earth. Keep in touch with them. You must all work together for the good of all whose lives you touch.

"Now, I'm about to end this letter, and you will remember all these things. Our adventures are not at an end; they are just continuing. Although we can never be apart, you will perceive me in different ways at different times. Always, *I Am*. Forever, *You Are*. Together, everything is possible. Remember, I am with you always. My beloved child, I have loved you with an everlasting love." At the bottom, it was simply signed, "Your God."

I looked up from the letter and observed how quiet and peaceful everything was around me. A breeze started blowing, gently at first and then increasing in intensity. As I replaced the letter in the envelope, a single gust of wind, mightier than the others, whisked it from my hands. In vain I made a desperate effort to recover it, but it was too late. It spiraled a few feet above my head and then floated higher and higher, way above the trees. I strained to see it as it disappeared from sight altogether.

Gideon and Marla stood up. He threw his arm around my shoulder while she held my hand and said, "We love you, John. All is well. We'll see you soon." They walked down the stairs, waving as they left, and before I could blink, they were gone. For a while, I sat absorbed in the silence of the moment—a moment that seemed to stretch for all eternity.

* * *

There is an overwhelming peace within me now. There is also the stirring of a mighty wind that blows across my soul. Like you, I am a part of All That Is and All is a part of me. I know that my work with Gideon, Marla and others, my quiet times with God, my love for my children, my memory of Mardai and my growing into a better me will continue forever. Just as your journey home continues, so will mine. I know that I will see my friends and loved ones again and again. Content with that thought, I went back into the house and poured myself another cup of coffee.

ABOUT THE AUTHOR

A prize-winning scholar and award-winning author, JOHN HARRICHARAN is also a highly respected authority in the field of business evaluation and consultation services. Named "Businessman of the Week" and "Outstanding Young Man of America," he is a sought-after speaker and guest on numerous TV and radio broadcasts nationwide.